A Passion for Plants:
The Treseders of Truro

by
Suzanne Treseder

With a Foreword by
Sir Richard Carew Pole
President, Cornwall Gardens Trust

Alison Hodge

First published in 2004 by
Alison Hodge, Bosulval, Newmill,
Penzance, Cornwall TR20 8XA, UK
www.alison-hodge.co.uk
info@alison-hodge.co.uk

ISBN-13 978-0-906720-37-0
ISBN-10 0-906720-37-0

British Library Cataloguing-in-Publication Data
A catalogue record for this book is available from the British Library.

Edited by Edward Cheese
Designed and originated by BDP –
Book Design and Production, Penzance, Cornwall

Printed and bound in the UK by TJ International Ltd.,
Padstow, Cornwall PL28 8RW, UK

Front cover:	Tree ferns (*Dicksonia antarctica*) at Trewidden Garden, Penzance.
	(photograph: Christopher Laughton)
Back cover:	Treseder Catalogue no. 5.
Title page:	*Cupressus macrocarpa.*
Page 4:	*Cyathea dealbata.*

Contents

Dedication

Early in my childhood my parents agreed to separate, and my three brothers, Andrew, Philip and Paul, and I were brought up by our mother, Phyllis. Andy, being the eldest, was effectively the man of the household, and our mother gave us a wonderfully happy and loving childhood. Our future spouses would always remember her interest in them and their friends, and her 'open house' at our home, Breffit Cottage, in Truro. It is to the memory of both my mother and my brother Andy that I dedicate this book.

FIG. 573. CYATHEA DEALBATA.

Foreword

By Sir Richard Carew Pole,
President, Cornwall Gardens Trust

It gives me great pleasure to write the Foreword to this splendid book, which tells the story of the Treseder family.

A Passion for Plants provides a horticultural biography of the Treseder family of Truro: five generations of Cornishmen who influenced horticulture to a considerable extent in Cornwall as well as world-wide. The family were instrumental in introducing commercially the well-known tree fern (*Dicksonia antarctica*) into this country; planting public gardens in Australia; introducing a number of new named plant species to the horticultural world (some of which were granted the prestigious RHS Award of Garden Merit), and changing the landscape of Cornwall with their planting and garden design.

Suzanne gives an insight into the emigration of a Cornish family to Australia; their discovery of new seeds and plants in Australia, and distribution throughout the world; their subsequent return to Cornwall, and the re-establishment of their nursery in Truro.

This book will be of interest to both horticulturists and Cornishmen, and readers will find some fascinating information within its pages. It is only due to dedicated horticultural families such as the Treseders that we can today experience and enjoy the wonderful gardens and plant species so readily available within Cornwall.

Richard Carew Pole

Treseders' third seed list: early twentieth century.

Acknowledgements

A Passion for Plants: The Treseders of Truro is a horticultural biography that has been a labour of love, particularly so as I have had no horticultural training. My somewhat limited knowledge of plants has increased considerably while I have been researching and writing the book, but I apologise for any technical errors in the description of plants that may remain. The project has given me a tremendous insight into my family and their passion for horticulture, and the opportunity to put down on paper some of the information about one branch of the Treseder family and its legacy for future generations.

There are many people whom I need to thank – those who have given me information, have inspired me to write this book, and have assisted in preparing it for publication – but, due to the great number of people who have contacted me with information in the course of my research, I have undoubtedly forgotten to mention someone! However, I wish to take this opportunity of thanking everyone who has helped me, in particular: Barry Champion, Head Gardener of Trelissick Gardens, who suggested that I write a book; David Knuckey, late of Burncoose Nurseries, who started his horticultural career with Treseders' Nurseries; Alison O'Connor and Bryan Badcock, who were also employed at Treseders' Nurseries; Joyce Lilly and her sister, Norma Miners, who lived at the Nurseries in the 1920s when their father was manager; Mrs Aubrey Cocking, and my sister-in-law, Marina Caton, for valuable information about my brother Andrew. I am indebted to Douglas Ellory Pett, author of a number of inspirational Cornish horticultural books, for his very personal interest in my project, his invaluable technical knowledge, and general kindness in assisting me to prepare the manuscript.

I would also like to thank the following people for their interest and encouragement: Alison Clough, Head Gardener at Trewidden Garden, Penzance, and her father, Peter Clough, former Head Gardener at Tresco Abbey Garden; Mark Brent, Head Gardener at Lamorran House Gardens, St Mawes; Marshall Hutchens of Duchy College, Rosewarne; Andrew Tompsett, Michael Farmer, and Barry Johns, who used to work at Rosewarne; F. Julian Williams of Caerhays; Lord St Levan, formerly of St Michael's Mount; Mrs Joan Jardine-Brown; Terry Underhill; Geoff Carveth; James Whetter; Mike Couch; Hugh Allen; the 'Q' Fund, Cornwall County Council; the late H.L. Douch; Jacquey Visick; the Royal Cornwall Museum for allowing the reproduction of the photograph of the Wardian case; James Hodge for the photograph of the churchyard at St Just-in-Roseland; Pat Ward for the photograph of Neil Garland Treseder; Sir Richard Carew Pole, for kindly agreeing to write the Foreword; Stuart Parker, and my daughter, Veryan.

Finally, my special thanks to my husband, Philip, for being a computer widower night after night; for helping me to organize my book, and for giving me the courage to finish it and get it published.

Suzanne Treseder
Playing Place, Truro
August 2004

1   A Cornish Family's Passion for Plants

Introduction

'Passion' is the only word which expresses adequately the horticultural instincts and ambitions that my paternal family, the Treseders of Truro, have inherited for over six generations, from the early 1800s to the present day. Travel along Cornwall's winding country lanes, and you will come across towns, villages, or hamlets that owe their now-familiar horticultural scenery to the once-famous Treseders' Nurseries of Truro. Whether it be the magnificent spiky outline of *Cordyline australis* (dracaena), with its superbly fragrant flower-heads; the tall, dark, gaunt, majestic trunks of the mop-headed *Pinus radiata*, or the numerous gigantic, craggy trunks of *Cupressus macrocarpa* commanding the skyline as you enter the seaside resorts of Bude, Falmouth, Fowey, Helford, Looe, Newquay, Penzance, St Ives, and St Mawes, remember you are looking at specimens planted mainly in the late 1890s by the Treseders.

Treseders' Nurseries undoubtedly made one of the greatest impacts on horticulture in Cornwall in particular, the south-west of England in general, and, to a certain extent, the rest of the world during the late nineteenth and much of the twentieth centuries. Little has been recorded of this single-minded, talented horticultural family, whose immense knowledge of all aspects of the wonderful plants they cultivated inspired many ordinary people to have beautiful informal gardens to provide year-round colour and interest. The Introduction to an early Treseders' catalogue (*c.* 1900), reproduced on page 10, captures something of the family's passionate enthusiasm for their trade.

The rare plants that the Treseders propagated at their nurseries were of the finest quality – among them, the first commercial introductions of Australasian and international plants with which John Garland Treseder had been familiar during his time as a nurseryman in Sydney, Australia. These included tree ferns, cordyline, phormium, eucalyptus, mimosa, and pittosporum. As the plant hunters returned from their

> *"There is an art*
> *Which doth mend nature – change it rather,*
> *The art itself is nature."* – Shakespeare

There is nothing new under the sun; and we cannot hope to say anything that has not often been expressed on the delights of Gardening. But though the theme be old, it is like verdant Nature itself – ever fresh. By gardening we do not mean the prim, formal style often seen, but the transferring to our own doors of the unfettered graces of Nature – as well as her rude magnificent features; as her most delicate and placid phases. This is the fount from which we would draw our inspiration, a taste inherited from our first parents, Gardening has ever been a favourite pursuit with all peoples – Englishmen especially love it, and hence the floral beauty of so many rural homes in this country – the result, be it remembered, of devotion to horticulture for ages. The exquisite bloom of some of our gardens attest what may be accomplished, and in a land so favoured as the West of England, with a soil so rich and an atmosphere so pure – where the reward is so handsome for such little labour.

Gardening is one of the pure, healthful joys which Nature places within our reach, revealing at every step her infinite graces and wondrous laws. At once refining and ennobling, it stands pre-eminent as a means of relaxation, and can be shared alike by the highly cultivated as by the unlettered. Here in this common field of nature, gentle and simple meet on equal ground, the patrician of the soil can glean no more satisfaction from his stately groves than the humblest labourer from his garden patch and the greatest minds in all ages have relished this fascinating art.

From the Introduction to Treseders & Co., Nurserymen, Catalogue, c. 1900.

expeditions, so Treseders' Nurseries acquired increasing numbers of exotic new plant species that required years of dedicated care and attention by their gardening staff in order to become sufficiently established for selling to an ever-expanding list of notable clients, world-wide. Family papers include a letter from Vita Sackville-West at Sissinghurst Castle, in which she requests a catalogue and places an order for *Jasminium angulare*:[1] she names her brother-in-law, Lord St Levan of St Michael's Mount as her reference. In 1902, the nursery supplied a large selection of new Australasian introductions to the Earl of Ilchester for his famous Abbotsbury Gardens; and when Sir Peter Smithers, the world-renowned horticulturist and photographer, created a garden from the bare ground for his new home Vico Morcote on the slopes of Lake Lugano in Switzerland in the 1970s, stocking it with over 10,000 species and varieties of plants from all over the world, it was to Treseders' of Truro that he turned for many of the specimens.[2] Original Treseders' catalogues dating from the early 1900s still survive and are a joy to read, being as fine and informative as any present-day gardening book. Indeed, it is a pity that such comprehensive information is not always available with the plants currently on sale in the many garden centres up and down the country – perhaps the disaster of *Leylandii* hedges could have been lessened had the suppliers of the trees followed the example of the Treseders' catalogues and provided more detailed information. Even today, to mention Treseders' brings acknowledgement and recognition from professional horticulturists, many of whom still lovingly cherish, and frequently refer to, their well-thumbed Treseders' catalogues.[3]

Sources for the history

Since about 1850, many members of my paternal family have recorded occasional aspects of their fascinating horticultural experiences in letters, and it is these that have been the main sources of information for this book. After he retired from the family nursery in the mid-1980s, my father, Neil Garland Treseder, began enthusiastically to collect material from distant relatives to expand this Treseder family knowledge. One day, out of the blue, not long after his son Andrew's death, he sent me some bundles of old letters he had received from relatives across the Atlantic. These members of our family recollected, with amazing clarity, stories about the Treseders' early days as settlers in Australia in the mid-1850s, and some possessed aged diaries describing events in greater detail. They were from an era when it was fashionable to have large families, and these fertile Treseder families were no exception, frequently comprising at least ten children, so numbers expanded exponentially within a couple of generations, making it more difficult for

Neil to keep to his own direct line without getting side-tracked. This was just the start of linking up the pieces of an enormous jigsaw puzzle: when he died in 1996, Neil had merely joined parts of the straight edges and most of the corners. He left volumes of family correspondence, old photographs, nursery catalogues, documents, and early Royal Horticultural Society books, plus 16 suede-bound books of copy letters from his grandfather's nurseries, covering the period from 1890 to 1924. These previously hidden treasures contain the names of seed and plant species the family traded and propagated, and of the gardens and parks they designed and planted, both during their final years in Australia and then back home in Truro.

Ready to create more colourful interlocking jigsaw pieces, the documents in this time capsule literally lay at my feet, cluttering up my office, each one in complete disarray. I simply could not resist delving deeply and attempting to make some sort of sense of lengthy epistles, lovingly hand-written on the most delicate, tissue-like paper, and signed by elderly ladies with names such as Bella, Trixie, or Biddy. For hours at a time I found myself stepping back into the past, discovering my own family tree, fascinated by what made these people tick. It quickly became apparent that many Treseder men and women, past and present, had a passionate obsession with horticulture, possessing an infinite understanding of plants' habits and tolerances. Many owned, and some still own, nurseries world-wide. The internet has facilitated access to distant relatives in far countries, many of whom have helped to collate family history, making the overall picture of the Treseder family enormous indeed. With all this intriguing horticultural history bursting forth, I came to believe that, since this fascinating family puzzle needed to be completed, it would be of interest to a wider audience than just my own family. Alas, all family members involved with Treseders' Nurseries in Truro have long gone; but, as there is so much precious and hitherto unpublished information to share, I would like to think that there is sufficient here to stand as testimony to the importance of these enthusiastic, pioneering horticulturists, whose love of plants frequently came before that of food and family.

The early history
The name Treseder has been traced back to the early 1200s and the village of St Buryan on the toe of Cornwall between Land's End and Pen-

zance. There is still a settlement called Tresidder in the area (OS map ref. SW392 241), and within recent years there was a small exotics nursery nearby, owned by a Tresidder. It is thought that Treseder was the original family name, with variations such as Tresidder evolving in the Middle Ages when ordinary people could not read or write, and the parish clerk spelt a person's name as it was pronounced to him.[4] Edmu de Treseder was taxed one shilling and eight pence, and a Thomasine Tresseder was taxed ten pence, indicat-

James Treseder.

ing that they were a stage lower than middle class. At about the same time, in the village of Constantine, near Falmouth, Edmund Tresedyer was taxed one shilling and sixpence, while in 1523, in the same parish, Michael Treseder was assessed in goods valued at seven pounds and taxed three shillings and sixpence.

My story begins much later, in the 1790s, when a farmer, Peter Treseder, married one Julia Nancarrow. Peter lived at Laity, and his farm at Bridge, on the outskirts of Portreath in the parish of Illogan, near Redruth, still exists. The family was probably connected with Wheal Rose Mine at Scorrier, near Redruth, part of which is the Treseder Shaft. (By coincidence, Treseders' opened a branch nursery next to the family tin mine in 1963.) Peter and Julia had nine children – seven boys and two girls – all of whom married and about half of whom eventually emigrated to live in either Australia or America. One son, James, who was born in 1804, became a gardener, and was employed on a large estate, probably Cotehele near Gunnislake, up the Tamar from Plymouth. He fell in love with a young woman called Hannah Garland, whose family lived not far from his parents' home near Portreath. The young couple eloped to Bodmin, and were married by licence in the parish of Calstock in 1830, setting the pattern for the family's second name of Garland when they named their children.[5] As was the fashion at that time, the mother's maiden name was passed on to the sons. John Garland Treseder, James and Hannah's seventh child, passed his mother's name to his son Ira, and for four further generations the tradition has continued, through to my late brother Andrew's son, Timothy Garland Treseder, calling his own son Francis Garland Treseder. This tradition was also carried on by some of James and Hannah's other children, many of whom emigrated: there can be no doubt that there are Treseder descendants in various parts of the world still bearing the name Garland, who are perhaps curious to know where their middle name originated and why – so it is that family traditions grow and spread world-wide.

James and his two elder brothers, Stephen and John, who had also been training as gardeners, acquired their understanding of work on the land in harsh coastal conditions from Peter, their farmer father.[6] Family archives show that, as a young man, James served an apprenticeship as a gardener at Scorrier House, Redruth, under the Head Gardener, William Lobb, who was to become one of the nineteenth century's famous plant hunters, collecting plants in South America for James Veitch of Killerton, near Exeter. At a time when most of the young men in Cornwall were mining, fishing, or farming, the Treseders were already men with a passion for plants. The three Treseder brothers moved with their young families across the county to the mild and fertile village of Mylor, at the end of a sheltered creek roughly half-way between Falmouth and Truro. They wasted no time in establishing themselves as market gardeners and seedsmen, growing fine quality vegetables, fruit and flowers to sell at the weekly markets, another brother, William, managing their seed shop in Redruth.

The 1820s and 1830s saw a marked rise in prosperity, and an expanding commercial class. Falmouth was rapidly developing into an extremely wealthy port, with newly built terraces of elegant houses that still grace this lovely town today. The harbour and the River Fal were constantly busy with packet ships, and cargo vessels carrying away the ore from the mines and bringing in exotic goods from distant lands. Inland, mining villages and towns, such as St Day, Carharrack, Redruth and Camborne, were teeming with people, many working on the richest copper lode in the world, and the streets were bustling with incoming traders. Mining was at its peak, and the Stannary town of Truro was rapidly becoming a thriving banking and tin-smelting centre. By the mid-1830s, James and Stephen had become more successful and better known, so they moved to Truro to expand their market gardening outlets, their vegetables feeding the town's growing population. They soon established themselves as an invaluable part of the fashionable hub of an increasing number of wealthy landowners and businessmen who were becoming keen plantsmen. This move also saw the beginning of the Treseder involvement with local and national horticultural shows. In 1838, at the Cornwall Horticultural Society's twenty-second exhibition, James Treseder won first prize for the best basket of vegetables exhibited by a market gardener. At the next show he again won the first prize, and Stephen won awards for the best collection of dessert apples, best six calceolarias, best group of heaths, and best onions. The two brothers were keen to compete against each other and promote the names of their businesses. The 1841 census recorded them as 'business gentlemen': they were beginning to climb the social ladder.

Stephen and his family took up residence in the tiny hamlet of St Clement, which nestles in the valley of a creek between Malpas and Tresillian. On the St Clement tythe map of 1842 his market garden was recorded as 'Quarry Premises', with the owner J.S. Enys, from the great estate of Enys near Penryn, and the occupier Stephen Tresidder (the family name still being variously spelt). James had rented land for his market garden with a fine house at Trehaverne on the outskirts of Truro; but in 1839 the opportunity arose for James to establish his own nurseries in Truro by renting the gardens and properties at Moresk, previously leased from the Enys estate by Lewis Charles Daubuz, who was one of Cornwall's most prominent tin-smelters and owned the smelting works at Carvedras nearby. The advertisement for the Moresk Nurseries, published in the *Cornwall Gazette*, read:

FARM AND DELIGHTFUL GARDENS,

IN AND NEAR TRURO

To be LEASED, for a term of seven or fourteen years from Lady-day next, all those

WALLED GARDENS,

GARDENER'S HOUSE and other buildings. Plantations, and Shrubberies, for many years past in the occupation of Lewis

Charles Daubuz, Esq., whose well known taste and liberal ex-
penditure have justly entitled them to be equal if not superior to
any Garden in Cornwall. The Walls are covered with Fruit Trees
of the choicest kinds, and the ground well stocked and in the
highest state of cultivation. The Gardens, Plantations and Shrubberies contain about five Acres, are well sheltered and watered, lie
upon a slope, aspect south-west and within ten minutes' walk of
the populous and improving town of Truro and would form an
eligible investment for any person of sufficient capital to carry on
fruit and vegetable gardens on a large scale.

Also, for the like term of seven or fourteen years from

Lady-day next, all that

DWELLING-HOUSE

Stable, Barn, and other Farm buildings, and Five Closes of rich
Land, adjoining the above-mentioned Gardens, and occupied by
Mr Daubuz therewith. A river runs at the bottom of each field.
The whole premises are in excellent order and condition, and contain about fifteen acres statute measure. If required the Tenants of
the Gardens and Farm must be prepared with good security for
payment of the rents, &c.

TENDERS for leases of the above several premises, (the takers of
which will be expected to execute counter parts at their expense,
containing the covenants, conditions, and provisos inserted in the
leases of John S Enys, Esq.,) to be addressed free of postage to
Mr. WARREN, Solicitor, Truro, on or before the 23rd day of February next, to whom application may be made for further particu-
lars relating to the premises.

Dated January 9, 1839

With the lease secured, James, his wife, Hannah, and their six children
took up residence in the farm and gardens in the sheltered valley at Moresk, and rapidly built up his business. This was to become the base of
Treseders' Nurseries for nearly 140 years, and the move set the course
of James' family's future for many generations.

The Treseders at Moresk

Moresk, home of the Treseders' nursery from 1839 to 1975, lies on the side of a valley that extends down to Daubuz Moors on the banks of the River Allen. This river, one of two that flow through the centre of Truro, supplied a mill leat dating from 1648. Last used by the Truro Steam Laundry, previously a mill, this watercourse is disused and dried up today, but follows the line of the original nursery driveway, and was the source of water for irrigating the stock for many years. Today a residential development called Treseder Gardens, the nursery site was originally the private leisure and produce gardens of the Enys family of Mylor, used by them when they stayed at the Mansion House, their home in Truro. The layout was of the type common to many large private gardens of the period, and included a walled garden equipped with a greenhouse on the south-facing wall, in which grew grape-vines and apricots. The red-brick walls created a microclimate with temperatures higher than those for the surrounding area, and there was a door in the wall at the bottom, leading on to the drive, which was opened when there was a frost to create an airflow that prevented the garden from becoming a frost pocket, thus protecting the more tender plants. The walled garden boasted all kinds of choice fruits and rare climbing plants trained against the walls, and produce beds planted with seasonal vegetables and soft fruit. One superb apple tree, called 'Waterford Non Pareil', although hollow, survived well into the 1920s, when it must have been over a century old. Eventually, a great gale blew it over so that it rested on one of the brick walls until it died. The site also included a grotto in the old quarry and the beech woods that climbed the side of the valley. One of James Treseder's first tasks on securing the lease was to remove many of the larger trees in order to give the nursery more light and provide room for planting stock. The Treseders' Moresk nursery is shown on the 1846 Duchy map of the manor of Moresk: it had groves, gardens and pathways, as well as some old pits not quite adjoining but near to the leat of Moresk mill, which were later developed as ornamental ponds.

In those days, transport and communication were slow and poorly developed. Foreign countries had only recently been penetrated by the plant hunters and, consequently, the varieties of species commercially available in Cornwall were limited to hedge shrubs, such as aucuba, privet, laurel, yew and box, and old varieties of roses. However, con-

THE NURSERIES, TRURO.
JOHN TRESEDER,
𝔑ursery & 𝔖eedsman.
Pleasure Grounds laid out, and Forest Planting executed by Contract, or otherwise.
BRANCH ESTABLISHMENT AT REDRUTH.

An advertisement for the nursery in Kelly's Directory, *1873.*

siderable growth of interest in ornamental horticulture soon followed economic growth, part of this interest involving the restoration of a landscape made barren by mining and smelting. Due to the need for charcoal as fuel for the smelting of tin, Cornwall had been denuded of many of its trees. Although coal was used in the smelting process at this time, there was still a need for timber in the mining industry, so much so that timber was being imported. The influence of Loudon and his *Encyclopaedia* and *Gardener's Magazine*, followed by the great *Journal of Horticulture* and the *Gardeners' Chronicle*, was moving horticulture away from the aristocracy to the middle classes, and developing a strong interest in tree species rather than the fashion for landscape gardening that had dominated in the eighteenth century. There were many wealthy mine captains and landed gentry with town houses and country estates, to whom James Treseder sold vast quantities of mixed woodland saplings, mostly native varieties, and hedging shrubs. Although the propagation of horticultural exotica was still in its infancy, this departure marked the first move away from market gardening towards a specialist nursery.

Tin ore mined in Cornwall was being transported to south Wales for smelting. Stephen owned a number of sailing ships and, from time to time, made the voyage to south Wales to expand his business interests. He soon realized the enormous horticultural opportunities open to him there and, before long, moved with his brother William to Cardiff, where they each established their own nurseries. For many years, Stephen Treseder & Son Ltd. proudly used the Cornish coat of arms and motto 'One & All' as its trademark. In time, William's son Fred made the name Treseder internationally famous for dahlias, raising and introducing a great number of new varieties during his lifetime, most notably the famous purple-leaved *Dahlia* 'Bishop of Llandaff', which was awarded the distinguished RHS Award of Garden Merit in 1928. He was also one of the founder members of the now famous 'Flowers by Telephone Company', Interflora. Stephen and William's move to Wales created the Welsh branch of the Treseder family as distinct from the Truro Treseders (with a different pronunciation of the surname).

James retired in 1881, aged 74. All of his sons had emigrated to Australia, so the lease of the Truro nursery was relinquished. The property was taken over first by Henry Browne, who was shortly declared bankrupt, and then by William Henry Hall, who announced the fact in the *Royal Cornwall Gazette* of 27 January 1882. Thus, for a few years, the connection of the name 'Treseder' and 'Nurseries' in Truro was severed, until John Garland Treseder returned to England in 1897, having spent nearly 30 years in New South Wales in the nursery business.

The growth of a family business

Until the early 1920s, Treseders' catalogues included numerous impressive photographs showing their nursery grounds bursting with subtropical Australasian plants, including striking tree ferns and palms, that were well established and thriving in the Moresk valley. Customers were encouraged to call in and enjoy these convivial surroundings at their leisure. This suggestion was clearly successful as, with the increasing popularity of the motorcar, many wealthy and horticulturally inclined clients began calling at the nursery in person to select the plants for their gardens, rather than leaving the decision to their gardeners: there was great excitement when the Duke of Bedford, of Endsleigh House near Tavistock, arrived in his chauffeur-driven car. To accommodate these vehicles, Treseders' extended the turning area to provide 'a good motor turn in a central position', and developed a system whereby 'customers may have their orders executed and packed at once if desired'.

Up to the demise of the business, members of Treseders' staff were still packing and preparing freshly dug plants for visiting customers to take away with them, while the modern garden centres were creating a market for the masses. Sadly, over time, specialization was to be Treseders' downfall, as more and more people became do-it-yourself gardeners who demanded instant effect: they had little experience of horticulture, and even less knowledge of plants' habits and tolerances, choosing them by colour and the fashion of the moment. However, the newly mobile customers had the pleasure of wandering around the nursery grounds, experiencing at first hand the mature specimens of a rich and varied selection of subtropical and foreign plants growing in the nursery to provide material for propagation. Until then, these species had been enjoyed only by landowners with large private gardens, or chosen from the informative descriptions in the Treseders' catalogues. After the Second World War, many more ordinary working people visited the nursery, as it was within walking distance of the city centre, and it became a favourite place for people to enjoy on Saturday afternoons off in the days before the spectacular private gardens of Cornwall were opened to the public.

All of this led the business to move into large-scale plant production and garden design. For well over half a century, Treseders' Nurseries carried one of the largest collections of ornamental plants in the whole of the United Kingdom, and had a considerable export trade. They offered lists, on application, of camellias and water-lilies they could supply, and the range of plants in the catalogues of the early 1900s is impressive. Treseders' Nurseries stocked almost 70 hybrid rhododendrons, plus Indian rhododendrons (*Rhododendron arboreum*); 20 different bamboos; five species of tree fern; 20 different hydrangeas; almost 100 types of conifer, including *Pinus insignis* (*Pinus radiata*); nigh on 500 types of alpines and perennials; numerous varieties of climbing plants (including 43 clematis, 33 ivies, 10 jasmine, and 15 lonicera), and many different roses, of which 65 were climbing varieties, 88 hybrid perpetual, 55 tea-scented [*sic*], 11 noisette, 78 hybrid tea, plus sweet briars, China, and moss roses. In their fruit section they offered many varieties, among which were 50 varieties of dessert apple, 54 culinary apples, 22 peaches (dwarf, espalier, or fan-trained), 20 plums, and 38 pears – all these besides the palms, forest trees, bedding plants, greenhouse plants and more, which made up the rest of the stock. Their seed catalogue of the same period is illustrated with coloured paintings of sweet peas, of which seeds were available for almost three dozen varieties, along with seed of annuals and vegetables, as well as bulbs, corms and tubers. Their list of sundries is fascinating, with obscure items such as 'Fir Tree Oil Insecticides – Pure Dissolved Bones – Guano – a most nutritious plant food and stimulant – Tobacco Paper and Tobacco Powder', plus, of course, Pencils, Sticks, Wall Nails, Wood Labels, Flower Pots – in fact everything that was required by a gardener for his allotment or small garden.

By the middle of the twentieth century, Treseders' had established an extensive mail-order business, rivalling that of the nearest competitor, Veitch's in Exeter. Most plants were dispatched by rail: trees had their stems tied to a long, straw-covered pole, and their roots bound with wet straw or reeds, and then wrapped in hessian. Camellias were sent out in huge numbers, planted in pots of a felt-like material known as 'whale hide'. There was also a considerable international trade, and all plants for export had to be checked by the Health Authority. Treseders' exported to the USA, Mediterranean Europe, Switzerland, Korea, Russia, South Africa, Sweden and the Channel Islands.

The original packing shed was the focal point of the nurseries. It was a cavernous, draughty construction, receiving plants from around the site that were collected each day by 'dilly', a long, two-wheeled, wooden trolley. As the various plants were taken off the dilly and given to the packers, they were checked against the delivery list. The employees were expected to know all the English and Latin plant names by heart: mistakes were not allowed and not tolerated, and no man was employed unless he always carried a pencil and a budding knife. In those days, recycling was considered the norm and businesses generally were economical in the use of costly packaging materials. The nurseries saved and used packing materials supplied by the local fruit shops. These included barrels filled with chipped cork, woven wooden mushroom baskets, or orange and apple boxes, of which there were always huge piles awaiting use. Sometimes, the boxes would have come from the Royal Gardens, Windsor, still bearing the labels addressing them to the Queen at Windsor Great Park. The hessian linings of these boxes were of superior quality, and were used by the men to make 'towsers', the hessian aprons they wore every day to protect their clothes.

Adjacent to the turning area stood an old cob cottage, home to James Treseder and his family when he took over the nursery lease in 1839. This long, narrow property was built into the slope of the hillside and abutted the exterior side of the walled garden, into which the two glass-panelled doors of the living room opened. A century later, after Ira built his new home, Illawarra, at the entrance to the nursery, the central part of this cottage became home to the nursery foreman and his family, although one of the rooms was still used as the accounts office. Underneath the lower end was a huge store, used for apples harvested from the ancient trees in the orchard and later sold to shops in Truro. Access to the upper storey of the cottage was by wooden steps set into the side of the pathway leading to the top entrance of the walled garden. Here was the nursery office, managed, as I remember it, by my aunt, Miss Mary Treseder, Neil's eldest sister. The walls were lined with hundreds of wooden drawers, each one containing thousands of tiny seeds of varying shapes, all carefully weighed or counted before being sealed in little buff-coloured oblong envelopes and neatly labelled. Nearby were small brass scoops, a pair of scales, and a set of tiny weights ranged in order of size in a line. Above the drawers, the walls were completely covered with certificates, too numerous to mention individually and many quite faded, for gold, silver, silver-gilt, and bronze medals that had been awarded to the Treseders over the decades at both local and national horticultural shows. Before the installation of mains drainage the toilets comprised earth closets: the ladies' closet, in a wooden shed at the top of the nursery, had two wooden seats side by side! The contents were disposed of by spreading on the land.

Expansion and modernization

In the late 1950s, after more than 100 years on the site, the Treseders finally purchased the freehold of the nurseries from the Enys estate. This provided the business with the security needed to make viable investment in a costly and radical modernization programme: it was necessary to move away from the outmoded Edwardian conditions. The purpose-built packing shed was placed adjacent to a modern office-block, both buildings overlooking the customer parking area, so that all orders could be assembled and packed under closer supervision from the management. The installation of one of the first electronic mist units proved to be one of the greatest breakthroughs in the horticultural world as it provided regulated temperatures that promoted reliable cuttings, as opposed to the hit-and-miss results from the traditional greenhouse where the cuttings were sprayed at regular intervals but the temperature could not be regulated. This greatly enhanced the development and success of propagation, and augmented the output considerably: for Treseders', this investment was immensely important.

The nurseries boasted seven large greenhouses, two of which were heated by pipes supplied with hot water from the coke furnace. As young children, my brothers and I spent most Saturdays at the nursery, and I have vivid memories of the greenhouses and the moss-covered, raised walls supporting the beds for the pots inside. Greenhouses 1 and 2, near the potting shed, were for cuttings and clematis, admittedly not very exciting for a child, but number 3, near the coke-fired boilers, was the mist house, home to the semitropical plants. It was great fun to try to race from one end to the other without being caught by the mist sprayers. Number 4 was home to hundreds of thousands of cuttings: each of the tiny cloam pots in this greenhouse contained coarse, gritty sand, covered with a fine film of green slime. The pots were made at Lakes, Truro's local pottery, which is now the site of the Baptist chapel adjacent to Bosvigo school in Chapel Hill. Some pots for the cuttings were as small as 5cm across, increasing in size for transplanting outside as the plants became established. Broken cloam shards were used to line the base of these pots to ensure adequate drainage. Number 5 greenhouse contained pots and pots of camellias, which, by the mid-1950s, had become a speciality of the nurseries. This greenhouse always gave me the impression of an enormous green carpet of shiny leaves, all reaching for the light. Number 6 contained seasonal pot plants for Treseders' florist shop in Truro: before Christmas it would be a riot of colour and strange perfumes, crammed full with magnificent cyclamen, chrysanthemums, and the scarlet bracts of poinsettia. I adored the wonderful smell of this greenhouse, especially when, in the early summer, it was filled with geraniums whose leaves had exotic aromas when crushed – some the usual geranium scent, but others smelling of peppermint, apple or lemon.[7]

Number 7, the fern pit, housed enormous ferns – popular from the early days as conservatory plants – banana plants and mimosa. This place was dark, mossy, and rather scary to a young person: to enter brought a rush of excitement at the bizarre shapes, humid atmosphere, and the gently perfumed, fluffy yellow, ball-shaped flowers of mimosa, with its delicate, feathery leaves. I have an old photograph of a banana plant bearing fruit that Treseders' sold to Sharpitor in the early 1900s. To the rear of these greenhouses, terracing the gentle slopes of the hillside, were row upon row of cold frames. All built on site, they were a combination of wooden and metal structures with hessian or hinged, glazed covers, used for hardening off cuttings and to accommodate the small pots of rockery plants and succulents.

Climate change at the nurseries

The climate of Cornwall during the last two or three hundred years has not always been as mild and subtropical as we are used to today. The hot summers of the 1820s were followed by storms, and there were extremely cold periods in the 1860s and 1870s, capped by the blizzard of 1890. Treseder diaries of the late 1890s detail freezing cold and snowy conditions, often extending from early October through to the following May. At the turn of the century there was a mild period, but notable cold spells returned in the late 1940s and early 1960s. A newspaper cutting from 1903 in the family archives records that:

> Many new introductions of rare shrubs now growing at Mr
> Treseder's Nurseries, Truro, have withstood the extreme weather
> experienced of late, and though covered with frozen snow, the
> plants seem as happy as when growing in their native dells, proving
> once again the wonderfully favourable climate of Cornwall for rare
> shrubs. The new *Eucalyptus Beauchampiana*, which is quite exposed,
> had icicles eight inches long hanging from the branches without
> any unhealthy effect whatever.

These variations in the climate were a great problem to Cornish gardeners, not least the Treseder nurserymen with their stocks of exotic plants. They also had to cope with the additional problems caused by the building of railway viaducts close to the nurseries.

The Great Western Railway's mainline track crosses the Moresk valley on the largest viaduct in Cornwall. Designed by Isambard Kingdom Brunel, the original structure consisted of sturdy, stone-clad pillars, on top of which were huge timbers supporting the railway line. In 1900, this was replaced by the present stone-arched, granite-pillared viaduct, although the original piers were left *in situ* and can still be seen today. The disruption caused by the construction upset the Treseders' business for many months, and made the driveway impassable to visitors. To keep their business solvent, John and his sons Ira and Jack were forced to leave their nursery and travel about calling on prospective clients to obtain more custom. Compensation by the railway company came in the form of a meagre £20 for the loss of trade, plus a free train pass from Plymouth to Penzance in order for them to be able to travel to promote their business. But the new viaduct and the remaining original piers also had a long-term effect on the climate of the area, as they formed an obstruction that restricted the flow of air, effectively ruining the nursery's natural air drainage. The valley became a reservoir of cold air, creating an enormous frost pocket where, on nights and mornings of radiation frost, temperatures were much lower than the average for the district.[8] Treseders' were very concerned about this man-made climate change within their nursery and realized that, to avoid irreparable damage to their stock, they would have to provide winter shelter for many of their tender plant introductions not thought to be completely hardy. The Australian bush houses they had used so extensively in their Sydney nurseries to prevent the heat and scorching sun from ruining their stock plants proved equally effective in protecting the plants from the cold in Cornwall. These structures consisted of metal frames supporting outer walls and roof woven from leafy branches, lined internally with hessian, and were well insulated against extremes of temperature. The Treseders were thus able to turn the apparently disastrous super-cold chill factor to their own advantage, for they acquired first-hand knowledge of the greatly reduced temperatures that their plants could tolerate, and discovered that many were, in fact, far hardier than had originally been realized. If the plants survived a cold winter at Treseders' Nurseries in Truro, then it was certain that they would grow successfully far beyond the confines of the supposedly mild south-western peninsula. In those early days of horticulture, there were no reference books on this subject: these enthusiastic nurserymen were continually experimenting and pushing the limits of their plants' resilience to the British climate.

Notes

1 Vita Sackville-West refers to Treseders' Nurseries in her book *In Your Garden Again*.
2 Sir Peter Smithers refers to Treseders' Nurseries in his book *Adventures of a Gardener*.
3 Hugh Johnson, in *The International Book of Trees*, names the Treseders as great plantsmen, and Philip McMillan Browse, one of the originators of the Eden Project and Horticultural Director of the Lost Gardens of Heligan, mentions Treseders' rosemary introduction, *R. officianalis* 'Corsican prostratus' in his article 'Rosemaries', in *Pacific Horticulture*.
4 Even in the family records there are various spellings of the surname, and different pronunciations of the name 'Treseder': acquaintances in west Cornwall frequently refer to me as a 'Tresidder'.

5   Hannah's father, Thomas Garland, came from a poor background but eventually rose to the prominent position of mine captain. He was an ardent Methodist and local preacher, and donated money for the building of Bridge Chapel. The Garland family's slate headstones are to be found in Illogan churchyard.

6   John died in an accident on 9 August 1850, aged 45 years. The *Cornwall Gazette* report of the inquest states that he was returning home from a horticultural meeting in Redruth and, on reaching Falmouth, offered to be cox for the Mylor school's gig. On nearing Mylor creek, he agreed to change places with an oarsman, appeared to get cramp in his legs, toppled overboard, and drowned. Mylor church, which is situated by the Yacht Harbour, has a slate floor made from very old headstones. I recently discovered John Treseder's headstone, set in the floor of the bell tower at the rear of the church: an unusual feature is that it states his profession as gardener, as well as the fact that he drowned.

7   Maybe it is in my genes, as I can never pass through a garden without touching the leaves of the plants, and enjoying each one's special leaf aroma.

8   The effect on the climate of the viaducts on the Moresk Nursery is confirmed by Mark Brent, Gardener for the exotic Lamorran House Gardens at St Mawes, who lives at the entrance to Treseder Gardens. He confirms that he has had occasion to scrape ice off his car windscreen as late in the year as early May. It is of interest that it was a Treseder show exhibit of *Kunzea baxteri* that inspired Mr and Mrs Dudley-Cooke to decide to plant exotic plants at Lamorran.

2   John Garland Treseder, 1841–1923

Introduction

John Garland Treseder was born in 1841, in a cottage at Mylor Bridge near Falmouth. The remains of this cottage can still be seen in a small field across the road from the playing-field at the head of the creek. He was the seventh of 14 children and although his parents, James and Hannah, had moved to Truro a few years previously, it would appear that they returned to Mylor for Hannah to give birth to John and her next four children. I can only assume that this was to enable her to have the assistance of relatives and friends who lived in the village.

The mid-1800s were a time of great population movement. With the Australian and American gold rushes and the beginning of the collapse of the Cornish copper and tin industries, many thousands of Cornish men and women emigrated to Australia, North and South America, South Africa, New Zealand, and, to a lesser extent, other parts of the world. This great emigration has been referred to by Philip Payton, in *The Cornish Overseas* (1999), as the 'Cornish Diaspora'. The local newspapers were full of exciting and tempting advertisements offering free passages to foreign lands, with the prospect of great adventure and fortunes to be made. The British Government was looking to populate Australia, and there were widely advertised lectures on 'free emigration' held at public halls and public houses throughout the county.

Part 1: Australia, 1857–1895

In 1857, John, who was in his mid-teens, together with his two brothers, Thomas and Charles, left his family behind and joined a voyage to Australia on the *Eastern City*, in search of gold. His Great Aunt Biddy remarked in a letter:

> Fancy three boys in their teens, Johnnie, Tom and Charlie going
> out alone to that wild country, but there was nothing in England
> for bright, personable young men from working class families.

Charlie must have been a great family favourite, for all the Treseder girls who had baby boys named one Charles. He was the one
who wrote home regularly.

What an adventure the sea voyage, lasting for over 90 days, must have
been for those young men – a journey on a vessel crammed with hundreds of desperately poor people, each taking their minimal, often very
shabby, belongings to a new country in the hope of improving their lot.
The Treseder boys were fortunate in that each had been given £50 by
his father. When they arrived at Port Jackson, the three brothers were
among hundreds of immigrants on their way to Ballarat, New South
Wales, so they had no difficulty in finding the gold-fields. What gold
they found nobody knows: it was inadvisable to broadcast any luck.

Their father, James, had realized for quite some time that emigrants
ought to consider taking with them vegetable seeds in order to be able
to grow food, and he had already established a lucrative business selling securely packaged seeds to be taken to foreign lands. Before leaving
home, John had the foresight to pack some of these seeds in his bag.
Tom had laughed at the idea, but it proved afterwards that this was a
wise decision as vegetables were in very short supply. Although gold
was a great temptation, the Treseders eventually returned to doing what
they knew and loved best: they acquired some ground and became market gardeners to satisfy the demands of the growing immigrant population. In creating their own businesses in the fast-expanding settlements,
they found this manner of work more profitable, safer, and more reliable than the hazardous job of digging for gold.

Soon tiring of Ballarat, the young brothers made their way across
New South Wales to Bathurst. It was here that John Garland Treseder
met an attractive young woman, Mary, the daughter of Richard and
Mary Beauchamp, who was to become his wife and stalwart companion. It is fortunate that my great-grandfather was careful to record
events in his life, as was fashionable among educated people of that
time. He recorded the early pioneering days and his meeting with Mary
Beauchamp in his journal:

> To those acquainted with the early history of Australia, the huge
> Blue Mountains seemed for years an insurmountable difficulty in
> opening the vast resources in the West. Many parties had been sent
> out, and all failed to get across these mountains rising higher and
> higher. No sooner had they climbed one, but another still higher

was before them and not
only this but thick scrub
had to be cut away, so that
only a very short distance
could be travelled each day.

There were deep open-
ings in the rocks which had
to be bridged. Party after
party returned quite beaten,
and for a long time the
mystery of the beyond was
hidden, until Lawson and
Wentworth volunteered to
undertake it. Their offer
accepted, everyone was
looking for failure, but with
dogged determination they
pushed forward. Keep-

John Garland Treseder, 1912.

ing on the crown of the high ridges, ridge after ridge, gorge after
gorge these men had the joy of standing on the last Western ridge
and there opened to their wondering gaze the vast fertile plains
(now called Bathurst Plains) with a large river running through and
as far as the eye could reach the finest Forest Lands, with hill and
dale and stream, all as yet unexplored. This discovery was doubtless one of the greatest achievements as yet known in Australia.

They hastened to Sydney with their report and the Government lost no time in putting on a large body of men to make the
road, so that access could be had to this new found Country, but it
was a long time before even a path or a bridle track could be made.
In time a good road was formed right across so that horse and
bullock teams could be driven carrying all requirements to the new
Country and now the people began to flock with thousands of
sheep, cattle and horses into the new land.

Meantime, explorers were out and had discovered the Lachland
River with all its hundreds of miles of suitable land for sheep and
cattle. Then the Macquarie was traced for hundreds of miles, as
well as the Barron and other important rivers. You can understand
what a place of excitement Bathurst was at this time, thousands

Mary Beauchamp's early home in Australia, c. *1860.*

of people all bent on occupying some of the new land that the
Government had offered so liberally.

Amongst others came Richard Beauchamp with his wife, who,
by the way had met in early life with a sad accident. In her fond-
ness for wild horses she had ventured too much, and was kicked
in the face causing a great disfigurement, but as one has said, "Tis
the mind that makes the body rich". She was a Miss Vane. Her
brother, as well as the Melville family, came up to the new Country. Richard Beauchamp built a little cottage near the never failing
spring where Mrs Beauchamp had an outlet for her kindness of
heart in supplying the travelling public from their well, the only
one for many miles. I should have said that Hargraves had just
discovered gold not far from the Beauchamps' home.

The Beauchamp family had moved many miles into the interior
and had set up quite an establishment and this is the place where I
met Mary Beauchamp for the first time. I must pass the difficulties
attending an introduction to the parents as well as the Lady, not
an easy matter, but it was managed notwithstanding, it was a time
which can hardly be described.

The climax came, her Mother and Father were quite agreeable
provided they were satisfied with my prospects and the home

I had prepared. Mr Beauchamp came to us on a visit of inspection and stayed some days and was fully satisfied and nothing now prevented the happy union.

Not long after their marriage, however, John received a cable from his father, James, who was approaching 60 years of age, asking him to return home to Cornwall so that he could take over the family nurseries.

Coming home

On 16 August 1866 John and his wife commenced the passage from Sydney back to England, on board the famous American ex-tea clipper *Flying Cloud*,[1] landing in Plymouth 97 days later in mid-November. John's journal (from which the following is quoted verbatim) describes the hazards of his voyage – an experience typical of many emigrants in those days:

> Left Sydney Harbour August 16th 1866 with a light wind off the land. Nearly all the passengers were sick for two days, some for four days very light winds until the 23 inst off New Zealand, when we got a wind that carried us on at about 10 knotts an hour for about a day and a night then a dead calm for 2 days and it is now 3rd Sept we are still about 150 miles past New Zealand.
>
> Sept 29th – Tonight 10 o'clock we struck a large Ice Burge, on the starbourd bough. We had just gone to bed, the night was fearfully dark, so much so, that the Ice could not be seen until it almost touched the ship's side. I heard the Chief Mate cry out to the Lookout man – who did not understand him – what do you say – Ice on the Starbourd bough he cried nearly on us – and in a moment we heard a fearful crash on the bough of the ship – and loud crys to God for Mercy – The Prayers of the people were granted for the ship bore off gently and a few terrible lurches – scarcely any one spoke on bourd for a few moments. The silence was the suspence. It was awful – not a person knew the damage we had sustained, or whether the ship was sinking or not – and all that could be seen was an emence mountain of Ice – as high as the ship's mast.
>
> I got out of bed so fast as I could the first I met was the first Cabin Steward who came rushing in fearfully terrified, I said what is the matter – he said Lord have Mercy upon us as we are in the middle of a wall of ice. He had been sleeping in the forecastle

– and the shock had knocked him out of his bed. At this time
there was not a soul on bourd but thought we were going to the
bottom. Lamps were carried around the side of the ship and to
the joy of all no very serious damage was done to the ship. It had
carried away the cat head and had broken the strong timbers on
the Bough. What astonished all was that there was no injury done
below the copper or water mark. It had broken a part of the Stern
of the Ship as well.

When the damage was ascertained as well as they could under
the circumstances – the bilge was sounded – all was perfectly right
as there was no more made water than usual – I suppose a more
narrow escape than this have never been known, no one could
sleep that night – we all waited for the Break of Day, it seemed a
week, but at last it came, after hours of anxious watching. The ship
was again examined, and all was found to be right, no serious damage being done. The mate said afterwards he did not think there
was the slitist chance of saving the ship but did all in his power to
put the ship off. There was about a ton of ice on the forecastle.
This was 57 degrees South of the Equater after rounding Cape
Horn. Mary was so ill that at one time she was nearly gone, but
looking into my face seemed to say – I am very ill but do not re-
gret coming with you – not a murmer, and full of courage. …

At seven pm 24th we crossed the Line with a beautiful breaze.
Each morning we saw a ship and signalled to it a New York vessel
bound to South America.

November 9th – Rose early – there is a beautiful wind carrying us about 12 miles an hour – the weather is beginning to feel
pleasantly cool. In the morning we saw a small Brigantine from
one of the Western Islands going to Plymouth with fruit probably
oranges. During the day we saw two other ships but did not get
near enough to know what they were. About sun down some passengers went on the Forecastle and said they fancied they saw land
(one of the Islands). We were then going about 13 or 14 knots
an hour and Captain said by the chart at 12 o'clock we could not
be more than 60 miles from one of the Islands – however, with
standing this there was no one on the lookout. The Carpenter hap-
pened to go to the Forecastle for something about 7 o'clock and
he cried out Land ahead, and sure enough when we looked over

the waters we could see the land quite clear. We were going right into it. What a blessing it was a starlight night. Orders were at once to put the ship off and we escaped without any injure [*sic*] but was within 2 miles of the shore. It was fortunate the night was not dark, we should certainly have gone on the rocks, no doubt. This was one of the Western Islands called the Coroo. About 900 miles from the English Channel. Went to bed at 10 – in the night there was a Rat came down on the bed, we lighted the candle but could not see any thing of it.

November 10th 1866 Rose this morning to see a beautiful clear sky – and there, in a good fair wind carrying on at about 12 knots we are in 41–45 miles North lat all being well in about 3 days with this breaze we shall make the Lizard Lights – we are getting very tired of the voyage for altogether its been a very miserable trying time. This voyage has been extremely hazardous and terrifying.

John and his wife continued by train to Truro. When local people heard of young Mr Treseder's marriage to an Australian lady and met her, they expressed their surprise that she was white – many people assumed that a 'native of Australia' meant an Aborigine. (Later, the expression 'Australian-born' was used to refer to those who were not 'native'.) His father, James, gave the young couple a house to live in for 12 months, plus an allowance of 30 shillings per week. After that time he agreed by contract 'to give up all his Nursery and Seed business, such portion of the Nursery Stock as then may remain, and the two meadows called "Trehaverne".' The stock, for which John had to repay his father at £50 a year, was to be valued by two experienced men. His father gave him the greenhouse and the frame that he used for propagating plants. John had taken on a great commitment and wrote in his journal:

I do not even wish to mention our early struggles in England, having entered into rather large responsibilities in buying the business, all having had to be paid for with interest. In certain, we were short indeed, a very small cottage with mean furniture and by this time a little family, but no word of complaint the smile of my wife always of the true helpmate.

On his return to Cornwall, another significant event marked his life:

At this time there occurred the most important change in our lives, our conversion to God. When we were married we promised we would serve The Lord, but we were constantly slipping away. We really had no power within us to serve Him, but when we believed in Him really as Saviour and Lord and really received Him as such it was His power that kept us and has ever since. We were both converted to God on the same day. My wife first. She was so happy in receiving the Lord Jesus as her Saviour that one could tell by her looks her hope was unquestionable. She was anxious about me. She persuaded me to see the Missioner.

This religious conversion was to become a major part of John's life. He was greatly influenced by the strength and dynamism of the Methodist movement in Cornwall, and wherever he travelled he was to 'work through the Lord', preaching the gospel and endeavouring to improve the lot of the poor. In Truro Methodist Church there is a stained glass window dedicated to him.

During the ten years in which he worked with his father at their Moresk nurseries, John built up a reputation for supplying mixed native woodland trees to replenish stocks in the county and create much-needed shelter-belts, developing valuable and lasting relationships with members of Cornwall's landed gentry, including the Williamses, Foxes and Bolithos, many of whom were enthusiastic plant collectors. Diary material reveals that between 1866 and 1867 John sold vast quantities of young saplings to large country estates such as Trewidden, Trereife, Caerhays, Scorrier House and Burncoose.

One of John's earliest surviving nursery catalogues (*c.* 1906) contains a table for the number of forest trees required per acre, and advises:

Forest trees are specially grown to withstand the most exposed situations. Forest planting by contract has been for more than half-a-century a speciality with our Firm. Thousands of acres of beautiful woodlands are to be seen all over this county which have been planted by us, and it will be seen that an eye to the picturesque has always been given, hence it is that so many mansions are seen backed up, and nestled amidst foliage of varied hues. In our stock nurseries we grow abundant numbers of Alder, Ash, Beech, Birch, Horse & Spanish Chestnut, Cornish Elm, English Elm, Pinus Austriaca, Silver Fir, Spruce Fir, Larch, Scotch Lime, English & Turkey Oak, Poplars, Sycamores, etc.

The return to Australia

After about ten years in Cornwall, John was advised by his doctor to return to Australia, on account of poor health. By this time John and Mary had six children, ranging from 12 months to nine years of age. Acting on the medical advice he had received, he and his wife and children packed up all their worldly possessions once again and set out on the long and arduous three-month voyage to Sydney. Once back in Australia, John's first move was to locate his brother, Tom, who had established a nursery at Dobroyd, near Ashfield in Sydney. They decided to go into partnership, trading as Treseder Bros. After a few years this partnership was dissolved: Tom remained at Dobroyd, and John bought a property from a Mr Underwood in Alt Street, Ashfield, called Camellia Grove. So impressed was he with the quality of camellia bushes and rare shrubs stocked by the previous owner that he renamed his new acquisition Underwood Nursery. He started to raise stock at once, among which was a new variety of camellia that he named *Camellia japonica* 'Thomas Treseder',[2] and, in the course of time, created a thriving nursery business, with a shop in the Royal Arcade, Sydney.

During his short period in Cornwall, John had studied under Edward Kemp, the celebrated landscape architect and author of *How to Lay Out a Garden* (1850), a book 'wherein he adapted Joseph Paxton's methods for the suburban garden.'[3] This invaluable experience enabled John to introduce landscape gardening in Australia, eventually designing government parks and gardens throughout New South Wales and

John Treseder's letter head from the Underwood Nurseries, 1890s.

Victoria, and laying out many large, extravagant gardens for wealthy businessmen along the slopes of Sydney Harbour. Business was so successful that within ten years he was the owner of three nurseries, a shop, and a seed warehouse. Together with his brother Tom, he wrote the first book published in Australia on gardening in the colonies, entitled *The Garden: A Simple Treatise in Gardening Applicable to the Seasons of this Colony.* The book sold out rapidly and had to be reprinted.

John's thirst for adventure and plant discovery took him to Norfolk Island and Lord Howe Island, off the coast of Australia, where he collected hundreds of thousands of palm seeds. He built up a valuable relationship with these islands' settlers, setting them up in the business of collecting seeds and palm plants for export to his nursery in Sydney in exchange for building materials. At Lord Howe Island he established a great friendship with Francis, Edwin and Alfred Nobbs, who collected seeds on his behalf, and on Norfolk Island traded for many years with N.C. Thompson and John Quintall and his family. His orders comprised palms with such names as 'Curly Palm', 'Linca Kentia', 'Mountain Palm', and 'Thatchy Palm'. (Family documents do not reveal how or when these later acquired their botanical names.) He shared his love of the words of the Lord Jesus with the settlers and, in 1885, two of them, George and Catherine Evans, presented him with a beautiful, hand-crafted wooden walking cane, now proudly owned by his great-grandson (my brother Paul), accompanied by the following letter:

> This cane is a present to Brother John G Treseder by his affectionate brother and sister in the bonds of Christian love Geo. Evans and Catherine Evans. It is made from wood cut by John Adams of the "Bounty" on Pitcairn's Island. The handle of it is made out of the tooth of a Sperm Whale, the rings are made of different woods, brought from Pitcairn's Island.
>
> It is given to him as a memento of his visit to Norfolk Island and likewise of the hearty cheering influence his visit here had upon the Children of the King who are living upon this Island. And that Our Father in Heaven may ever bless him both in this life, and the life to come will always be the prayer of the Givers.
> Genesis 31st Chap 49 v.

On 27 August 1888 he wrote to Dr John Adams – who, it is interesting to note, was a member of the crew involved in the mutiny on the

Bounty – ordering the following seeds and cuttings: '10 Sacks Pine Seeds, 12lb Dracenia [*sic*] seeds, 1 case Dracenia cuttings, 2 Wardian cases, 100 Asplennia, 100 Maratia, 100 small palms, 100 small ferns.' John Treseder was particularly interested in a red dracaena that, on his return to Cornwall, he named *Dracaena tresederiana*. John Adams was also a man of God, and clearly there was a great and valuable religious bond between the two men.

The Wardian case from Tregothnan, Falmouth.

Wardian cases

Plant hunters who wanted to bring home live plants in the age of sail were handicapped by the difficulties of transporting them thousands of miles through different climatic zones in salty air over a period of months. Dr Nathaniel Bagshaw Ward (1791–1868), a physician from the East End of London, offered the first significant solution to the problem by producing the 'Wardian case', a kind of portable miniature greenhouse. These cases were sent abroad as flat packs, assembled in the field, and filled with soil and plants. The plants were then watered thoroughly, the moisture being drawn up through the roots and lost again through the leaves in the usual manner: as long as the case had enough light, the lost moisture evaporated, filling the case with vapour, which condensed back to water on the glass and ran back into the soil to keep it damp. The cycle repeated itself, and the plants thrived. The last known Wardian case still in existence is in Cornwall, at Tregothnan, near Falmouth, the home of the Boscawen family.[4]

Tree ferns

The tree ferns were named *Dicksonia* in 1785 by the French botanist Charles Louis L'Heritier de Brutelle, after James Dickson (*c.* 1737–

1822), a botanist, nurseryman, and founder member of the London Horticultural Society, now the Royal Horticultural Society, and the Linnaen Society. Loudon mentions tree ferns only once in his *Encyclopaedia of Gardening* (1824), when discussing heated conservatories: 'The tree ferns, Humboldt [a German botanist] informs us, are of singular beauty, in their native sites. Only a few species of these have been introduced.' This suggests that they were better known on the Continent than in Britain, and then only as stove plants (i.e. plants grown in heated conservatories).

Dicksonia comprises some 25 species, distributed in the Southern hemisphere, especially Australia, Tasmania and New Zealand, where it regularly withstands frosts and snow. According to Hora (1981), tree ferns grow under a tree canopy, where they receive little light, and can survive forest fires. In cultivation they require continuous moisture, the *RHS Dictionary* (1956) recommending that 'In summer the trunks ... should be thoroughly watered twice a day, the amount applied being reduced as the season advances, only enough being used to keep them moist during the winter.' The 'trunks' of tree ferns are technically rhizomes and, unlike the trunks of our native trees, are fibrous and without bark. The roots at the base are 'adventitious' (that is, additional or exceptional), their sole purpose being to stabilize the trunk-like rhizome, which can grow to a height of 10–12m. As with other ferns, the fronds grow from the top of the rhizome. All these details may seem academic; but the botanical features are of importance in the transport of tree ferns. John travelled widely in Australia, Tasmania and New Zealand throughout the 1880s, and introduced plants of native origin into the gardens he was designing. Thus it was that, during an expedition into the Blue Mountains, he became captivated by the splendour of the native tree ferns, *Dicksonia antarctica*, growing in the deep, shady gorges, and also discovered that these giants would grow again after being scorched in the frequent bush fires. The burnt fern trunks were far easier to transport than the growing specimens, and were quickly rejuvenated by being immersed in water for some days.

The skill of John Treseder – a skill he passed on to his descendants – was in recognizing the potential of a plant for use in ornamental planting. Although the tree ferns were known in Europe, and perhaps occasionally planted in conservatories, he recognized that they could survive out-of-doors in the mild, maritime climate of Cornwall, and, acting on impulse, he wrote to many of the estate owners whose grounds he and his father had provided with woodland trees during his previous ten years in Cornwall, suggesting that they might try out these new plants. Consequently, in May 1892, he successfully dispatched small numbers of *Alsophila australis* (*Cyathaea* [*Alsophila*] *excelsa*) and *Dicksonia antarctica* to Cornish estate owners such as Thomas Bedford Bolitho of Trewidden, near Penzance; Sir Arthur Pendarves Vivian of Bosahan on the Helford River; Jonathan Rashleigh of Menabilly, near Fowey; Miss Anna Maria Fox of Penjerrick, near Falmouth, and J.C. Williams of Caerhays, Gorran, St Austell. In May 1893 John wrote to Mr Sangwin, Head Gardener at Trelissick, near Truro, asking if he would be prepared to act as an agent for him to promote the sale of tree ferns in Cornwall. John's Australian nursery order-book reveals in particular that he also exported an enormous collection of various Australasian plants and seeds to Bosahan[5] and later, on his return to Cornwall, he contacted Sir Arthur Pendarves Vivian whenever he received a rare new plant species. His recognition of climatic similarities between Australia and his beloved Cornwall was rewarded with the successful importing of some of the first in a long line of commercial introductions of Australasian plants. In 1892–3, John also exported tree ferns world-wide, including well over 500 to nurseries in Philadelphia and San Francisco for newly wealthy American clients.

Legends have grown up about the introduction of tree ferns to Cornwall: one story has it that the trunks first arrived as ballast in ships, and were then seen by John Garland Treseder to shoot on arrival, leading him to realize the commercial potential of introducing the plants. Treseder papers neither confirm nor deny this, but John's letter books prove the commercial introduction of these plants to be otherwise. A letter to Sir Philip Fysh, Agent General for Tasmania, dated 14 December 1899, tells a different story and contains interesting details of some of the first commercial shipments of tree ferns to Cornwall after John's return to England:

I have been asked to give a lecture upon the subject of my twenty-eight years experience in Australia...

Instructions for packing and sending home the Tree Ferns.

The height should be from 5 to 6 feet [1.5–2 m]. The fronds must be cut away taking care not to injure the crown. They should be packed in cases which are a little longer, say 12 inches [30 cm] longer than the ferns to allow a little growth on the way. The stems should be packed in damp sawdust and soil mixed and care should be taken not to allow the sawdust to get within 8 inches [20 cm] of the crown, the case should be divided here, with a little moss or straw. Great care should be taken not to injure the crowns in bringing from the bush. They should be shipped the latter end of February or March and placed in a cool part of the vessel all the better if in the baggage room.

I brought mine home in that part of the ship and was very fortunate. If they can be landed in Plymouth, so much the better. When getting Tree Ferns it will be best not to cut them high up but they should be cut near the bottom – in fact all the better if below the surface.

In the early days there were restrictions upon the importation of exotic plants into the British Isles, due to a fear of disease being introduced. One former nursery employee relates that he was told by Ira, John's son, that John smuggled tree ferns up the Helford River by boat to be planted at Trebah. An extract from his wife Mary's diary, dated 3 June 1900, reads: 'Our tree ferns arrived this day. A very exciting time – unpacking – dipping and planting. One case missing. We believe it has been taken on to London.' Ten days later she writes: 'The tree ferns that were carried on to London came to hand this day. They have been dipped and are now being planted.'

An early surviving Treseders' catalogue, dated 1904, features a full-page descriptive advertisement for *Dicksonia antarctica* with a photograph of three medium-sized tree ferns in small pots relative to their size. The 1908 catalogue has a similar advertisement, but with the addition of four species of the related genera *Cyathea*, sometimes referred to as 'Sago Fern'. These are *C. [Alsophila] australis*, and *C. dealbata* from New Zealand, *C. [Alsophila] excelsa*, introduced in 1825 from the Mascarenes, and *C. [Alsophila] moorei*.[6] All of these are described as greenhouse or stove plants in the *Royal Horticultural Society Dictionary* (1956). Tree ferns were to become one of the outstanding features of the early Treseders' Nurseries, and the following extract from the 1911 catalogue shows that varieties other than *Dicksonia antarctica* were available at that time:

TREE FERNS – no description could do anything like justice to these wonders. They are so majestic, as to eclipse all, and stand out so distinctly that they seem to give a Royal dignity to the garden. They should be planted in half shade in sheltered nooks, in well arranged groups.

Dicksonia Antarctica has now proved itself to stand the climate of Cornwall and South Devon, and may now be had from us in any size up to six feet stems, well established in our Nurseries.

Alsophila excelsa – very fast grower, with immense fronds, grows well right exposed to the sun

Alsophila Moorei – a very ornamental variety

Alsophila Australis – Prickly black stem

Cyathea dealbata – The New Zealand silver Tree Fern

Prices on application

These tree ferns flourish to this day at Trengwainton, Trebah, Tregothnan, Trelissick, Menabilly, Port Eliot and Heligan, among many other places. Indeed, the superb collection at Trewidden, near Penzance, situated in what was once an open-pit tin mine, has been described as 'probably the best grouping of *Dicksonia antarctica* … in the Northern Hemisphere'. So suited is this pit to the species that the number of specimens has increased naturally, many having trunks of over 5 metres high, and graceful 2.5 metre-long fronds. The original plants even survived bombing during the Second World War. These wonderful Cornish gardens are now nearly all open to the public, and every year, hundreds of thousands of visitors are enchanted by their magical atmosphere.

However, with the approach of the First World War, sales began to decline: most large private gardens had already planted their tree fern groves, and the cost of importing the enormous trunks was rising. Eventually, in 1972, the Treseders' catalogue stated that as it was 'no longer economically possible for us to import mature tree trunks from the Blue Mountains of New South Wales, instead we offer immature specimens which have been raised from Treseder introductions of 80 or 90 years ago. There also have been restrictions under the "Trade in Endangered Species Convention", the present stocks of tree ferns coming from sustainable sources.'

International trade

In addition to amassing a huge range of plants and shrubs at his nurseries in Sydney for use in his garden designs, John realized that there was a lucrative trade in exporting seeds of the Australian native plant species, and set up a separate, extensive international seed and plant trade.[7] Without the benefits of refrigeration, however, it was extremely difficult to prevent the contents of the packets from either rotting or germinating *en route*, due to the high humidity during the lengthy sea voyages. The palm seeds were therefore packed in a mixture of saw-dust, earth, and charcoal powder, and kept in a slightly damp condition in small tin canisters packed in wooden cases. By 1890, John had cir-culated notices of his export business to all of the principal wholesale seed firms and major pot-plant raisers in England, France, Russia, Bel-gium, Hong Kong, Cape Town, Java, Italy and Japan; and in America, those in Chicago, New York, Philadelphia and San Francisco. He es-tablished an important connection with Charles Ford of the Botanic Gardens, Hong Kong. However, John did not confine his interest solely to exporting his seeds world-wide: wherever he sent seeds, he requested that he should receive, in return, samples from the plants native to the destination countries, so that he could attempt to grow them in the wonderful Sydney climate.

Over half a million palm seeds, at a value of some £700, were ex-ported in May 1891. In July of the same year a further half million seeds were sent to South Africa, America, Europe and England, on the SS *Lusitania*. These were chiefly of *Rhopalostylis baueri*, *Hedyscepe can-terburyana*, *Howea belmoriana*, *H. fosteriana*, *Kentia moorei*, and *Ptychosperma elegans*. An order of 35,000 assorted seeds was sent to Thos. Rochford in Hertfordshire, which was to become England's greatest producer of house-plants. This order cost Rochford's the princely sum of £45.5s.9d (about £45.30). However, they obviously benefited from their purchase of these exotic palm seeds: their next order was considerably greater, comprising some 150,000 seeds. The Treseder seed business had be-come truly immense, as John's customers were always eager to obtain new and unusual plants. The seeds of *Archontophoenix alexandrae* became available in June that year, when about 4,000 were exported to England and even Calcutta, followed by 10,000 *Corypha australis*. In July 1892, Treseders' shipped 13,000 *Araucaria columnaris* seeds, 500 of which went to Curtis & Sandford of Torquay. Initially, trade with England specifi-cally involved the seeds of Kentia palm and Norfolk Island pine (now known as *Araucaria heterophylla*, which has been awarded the RHS Award of Garden Merit), both of which became very popular house-plants, a popularity enhanced by the fashion for conservatories. John had also germinated some of his Norfolk Island pine seeds, and in April 1893 he was exporting these as seedlings, Messrs Rochford being sent 1,000 in three Wardian cases. With millions of seeds being exported world-wide, together with vast numbers of tree ferns and palm trees, by September 1892 John had accounts of almost £3,000 due from export shipments through his London agents, Watson & Scull.

As John Treseder's reputation grew, the Australian Government sent him on many important assignments to assess and improve the Aborigine station at Camarragunga. He was very concerned at the lack of adequate sanitation and the high incidence of typhoid; but, at the same time, he was able to undertake a great amount of evangelical work within these communities. There were vast, uncultivated and uninhabited tracts of land, the potential of which John noted in one of his reports: the fertility and climate of these areas were ideally suited to the growing of fruit trees. He was soon importing many new varieties of fruit tree from France for these regions, which have since become major fruit-growing areas in Australia. In 1888, besides the fruit trees, John's nursery stocked 18 different varieties of grape. The production of fruit stock gradually began to make up a fair proportion of a lucrative two-way trade with France. In January 1892 he exported 200,000 fruit stocks, comprising almonds, apples, plums and pears, to Messrs L'Atellier & Son [*sic*] of Caen. The following year, 100,000 cherries, pears and apples were exported to A. Charoze of La Pyramid: it would appear that John Treseder may have been partly responsible for building up the fruit-growing industries not only in Australia, but also in France.

Yet despite the fact that the nurseries in Australia were flourishing, there was to be a change in the economic fortunes of the country: Australia suffered a huge financial crisis, caused, in part, by a maritime strike. John's trade in exported seeds became paralysed, and his customers found that they could no longer obtain plants for their gardens or afford many other luxuries. In 1895, at the age of 91 years, John's father, James, died in Cornwall. By coincidence, the former Truro nursery at Moresk (which had changed hands when James retired) became vacant. John at once cabled his sister and cousin, requesting them to retrieve the lease and employ labour to keep the Truro nursery in order while arrangements were made for his homeward voyage to Cornwall.

Within six months, at the age of 54, John had returned to Truro and a new chapter was to open in his life.

Part 2: Cornwall, 1895-1923

At the time of his father's death and his return to Cornwall in 1895, John Garland Treseder had already spent nearly 30 years in Australia. His horticultural knowledge had been unique and innovative, his landscape designs imitating many pretty woodland scenes he had experienced and marvelled at on his travels in the Blue Mountains and to Norfolk and Lord Howe Islands. These were productive years during which he had built up a flourishing business and gained a great deal of experience which was to prove of enormous benefit to him on his return to the family nurseries in Cornwall. His training in garden design had resulted not only in private commissions and engagements by the Australian Government, but also in his advice being sought as to the planting of some of the great estates in Cornwall. His interest in and experiments with new and exotic plants had developed into a broadening, reciprocal, world-wide trade in seeds. This, combined with first-hand practical knowledge of the climates of Australia and Cornwall, provided him with a unique understanding of the potential for the introduction to Cornwall of a wide range of new and unusual plants and innovative ideas, at a time when many garden owners were eager to possess new plants, and during a period when the Cornish climate had entered one of its milder phases.

Setting up the nursery

Unfortunately, the old nursery was very run down and neglected; but with what labour was then available, John was gradually able to return it to order. The following year he was joined by his wife, Mary, and their two unmarried daughters, Annie and Hannah, who travelled second class with the Orient Steam Navigation Company to Plymouth, at a total cost of £74.4s.2d (about £74.21). One of John's first plans was to enlarge his range of plants at the Truro nurseries by importing the more hardy exotics he had been used to growing in Australia, and he gradually introduced these species into the gardens he was commissioned to lay out in Cornwall. These Australasian plants included eucalyptus, mimosa, palms, pittosporum, phormium, and, of course, tree ferns. John was an enthusiastic and energetic businessman, and was welcomed by his father's customers. His nursery order-book shows that, within two years, he had re-established accounts with many of the Cornish gentry, some of whom, according to his letter books of the late 1880s, had also been his own clients when he had nurseries in Australia. As his reputation spread, he was asked to give lectures on his experiences as a nurseryman in Australia and the plants that he was now introducing.

It is clear that John Garland Treseder was influential in horticulture world-wide. The narratives of the Australian episodes, and the statistics from his letter books highlight this importance; but his period in Cornwall from 1895 to 1923 is epoch-making, and his great contribution to horticulture in this county needs to be appreciated.

Continuing relations with Australia
From Cornwall, John continued the international export trade in seeds and plants he had established in Australia, but now the direction was reversed. A good example is the relationship he had built up earlier in his career with Sir Philip Fysh, Agent General for Tasmania. Originally, Sir Philip had helped John to import tree ferns to England, but in November 1899, John wrote to him suggesting that the

> Time has now arrived to send plants and trees to Tasmania and if you will favour me with the time I will give it my most careful attention, as I mentioned in my former note there are many things which you could with advice introduce into your Colony.
>
> The enclosed little list of Cannas are for tropical effect in your gardens. I could send many plants and trees, which are entirely new to the Colonies and which would be quite hardy and thrive well in Tasmania.
>
> Now I am desirous to serve you and it is for you to say in what way [*sic*] your Public Gardens in Hobart are so beautifully situated, and are full of visitors, increasing every year – you may see your way in the interest of the Colony to increase the attraction in this way.
>
> Waiting for your kind reply,
> I have the honour to be your obedient servant.

In order to foster this profitable relationship, John arranged for Sir Philip to visit the beautiful holiday resort of St Ives, so that he could experience for himself the climatic similarities of Cornwall and Tasmania, and also see the wonderful new plants Treseders' was successfully introducing throughout the county. In this way, a substantial export trade was established from Treseders' Nurseries to the Botanical Gardens at Hobart in Tasmania, and, in exchange, copious numbers of Tasmanian tree ferns were sent to John at Moresk by way of payment.[8]

Protective planting and wind-breaks

The Pacific gales and salt winds in Australia had given John and his sons the opportunity to observe which plants were most suited to exposed, maritime gardens. The rough, wind-swept coasts of Cornwall and Devon presented a similar challenge to John's expertise: it was obvious that, in spite of the mild climate, nothing ornamental, exotic, or tender from Australasia would grow without adequate and suitable shelter. He therefore produced huge quantities of hedging plants, such as escallonia, *Fuchsia riccartonii*, veronica, and olearia, for use as salt-tolerant windbreaks, while wattle hurdles were imported from Somerset to be used as outer protection on the more exposed sites. John initiated the wider use of the fast-growing *Pinus radiata*[9] (the Monterey pine from California) and *Cupressus macrocarpa*, which he had grown to great effect as shelterbelts in Australia. During his travels, John had noticed that these trees were being widely used in New Zealand as shelter, to replace the huge swathes of trees cut down for building and fuel by the massive population of immigrants. The 'New Zealand method' had been developed to overcome the difficulty of transplanting safely such fast-growing species of tree. Having used it so successfully while in Australia, John was encouraged to propagate similar shelter trees in vast quantities by this method to plant throughout Cornwall and the milder regions beyond.

The New Zealand method, described by John's son, Ira, in a catalogue dating from *c.* 1913, involved transplanting the seedling trees annually, each spring, in order to promote a compact, fibrous root system without the tendency for tap-roots to develop and coil as they do when young trees are grown in pots. This enabled reliable transfer to more distant sites when the trees were five or six years old and quite large. They were lifted several months prior to their sale, and the roots enclosed in hessian tied with fillis [*sic*] twine – a process known as 'balling'. The trees were then replanted until the roots emerged through the hessian covering, subsequent removal of the cloth being unnecessary as it rapidly decomposed.[10] In mixed woodlands, these fir trees were thickly planted along with elm, poplar, sycamore and ash, forming effective wind-breaks throughout the south-west. Many of the extensive original plantings of these magnificent pine trees, which can still be seen around the county today, were raised from seedlings at the Truro Nurseries. John Garland Treseder's enthusiasm and dedication in encouraging private landowners to plant these fast-growing, wind-tolerant, evergreen trees and shrubs in their gardens, continued by his descendants, has had a dramatic impact on the Cornish landscape. Most of the surviving Treseder specimens of *Pinus radiata* are now well over 100 years old, but still stand out prominently on the Cornish skyline, their mop-heads supported by tall, stark trunks, from which the lower branches have dropped in the course of the trees' maturity. Sadly, many are past their prime and are now dying. However, it is interesting to note that, in the 1960s, the Forestry Commission was raising considerable quantities of *Pinus radiata* for planting out on its forestry trial grounds on the exposed Lizard peninsula.

Treseders' Nurseries had proved that, having provided the initial shelter, it was possible to grow many of the rarer and choicer plants in situations where previously it had been considered folly to attempt their cultivation. The family's expert knowledge concerning the protection of the beautiful, tender, exotic species encouraged the fashion for wealthier people to build residences with gardens on exposed sites in coastal situations – the gardens at Willapark, Tintagel, and at Trewoon, Mullion, both dating from the early 1900s, were two typical examples of these achievements. The unique case of St Michael's Mount, exposed on all sides to the ravages of salt-laden gales, is perhaps one of the most outstanding examples of the planting of salt-resistant trees as wind-breaks. In a letter of 1899 addressed to Piers St Aubyn, John wrote:

> Sometime ago Lord St Levan expressed a wish to do some planting of very hardy ornamental shrubs in groups on the Mount and to do a few improvements by way of experiments.
>
> There are many plants which we have found to stand such a position and if planted with judgement should go a long way to make the appearance of the Mount more interesting – Mr Treseder will be at Marazion in a few days and will do himself the honour of waiting upon you on the subject.

Etchings of the Mount from before this period show that it was devoid of trees and shrubs, but during the next four years Treseders' supplied Lord St Levan's gardener, Mr Holmes, with wind- and salt-resistant plants such as *Pinus radiata*, *Cupressus macrocarpa*, English elm, phormium, and *Olearia fosterii*, making possible the beautiful and exciting gardens which visitors enjoy today. In 1901, Treseders' also provided Mr Dorrien Smith of Tresco Abbey on the Isles of Scilly with such shelter trees. At around this time John was also engaged to visit the head gardeners at Trewidden and Trengwainton near Penzance, estates owned by the Bolitho family, with whom he had close professional contact. He checked their plantings of woodland trees and groves of tree ferns regularly, and, in return, was given permission to take cuttings from their rare and special plants to propagate at his nurseries in Truro, since in those days no one else was propagating such plants on a commercial basis.

Evangelism

In writing of the achievements of John Garland Treseder, it would be remiss to ignore his evangelistic fervour, his conversion to Methodism on his first return to Cornwall, his religious work in Australia, Lord Howe, and Norfolk Islands, and his concern for and care of the Aboriginal peoples. His experience of poverty in Cornwall led him to contrast the condition of local people unfavourably with that of their Aboriginal counterparts. In a letter of 1899 to the Cornish philanthropist J. Passmore Edwards he commented:

> Some time ago I wrote to you on the subject of houses for the poor of Truro. You were good enough to reply and now I am again taking the liberty to write to you on the same theme. I feel certain if you were led in this direction in the most simple way, much could be done – at present the poor people there are not considered, many of them live in places which are utterly unfit for any human being. There are lovely fields around Truro where cottages for these poor souls could be built.
>
> I have been much in Australia where I declare to say the Aborigines are in a far more happy situation – they had at least the advantage of pure air. Our lovely county far surpasses – to my mind – any other place in the world and our people are as a rule very thrifty – many are however through force of many circumstances

rendered helpless and they need the thoughtful wise sympathy of their brothers.

With his commitment to Christ, John was busy as a local preacher in the Methodist Church, travelling weekly to many country chapels between Truro and Redruth. He was also instrumental in arranging for ministers to visit Cornwall and, in some cases, was responsible for assisting in the costs of their travel to the county.

Treseder & Co.

Up to this point we have concentrated upon John's return to Cornwall and his work to re-establish the Moresk nurseries. But what about the nurseries in Australia? The urgent need for John to return to the homeland on his father's death had left him little time to settle his affairs in Sydney, or even to arrange for his wife to join him until a year later. The nurseries were, therefore, left in the care of his two sons, Jack Bathurst and Ira Garland, who were already experienced horticulturists. It took them about four years to wind down their father's Australian businesses, during which time they secured trade contacts for the export of the numerous Australasian plants for the Moresk nurseries in Truro. By 1902 the two brothers and their young wives were able, at last, to cross the world to join their father in Cornwall.

John, Jack and Ira now formed a partnership, trading as Treseder & Co., and continued to test the hardiness of supposedly tender exotics in their Truro nursery. Gradually, their new range of exotic plants, which included acacia (mimosa), eucalyptus, lapageria, callistemon (the 'bottlebrushes'), melaleuca, grevillea, pittosporum, leptospermum, and cordyline (dracaena), were produced on a commercial basis and sold to gardens and nurseries throughout Cornwall and sheltered localities further afield.[11]

A new style of garden design was in the making. In one of the earliest surviving Treseders' Nursery catalogues (*c.* 1902), John, with the assistance of Ira, encouraged customers to look at and assess their gardens from a completely different, less formal angle, with the following new suggestions:

SUB TROPICAL EFFECTS

In these days of travel, when it is so easy comparatively to visit scenes which are altogether distinct from anything English, we naturally wish to produce something in the home garden that reminds us of what we have seen in other regions. We have found that most beautiful effects can be produced by somewhat altering the level and formation of the ground in a natural way and by the introduction in the garden of Dracaenas in picturesque groups. These Dracaenas [*Cordylines*] are so entirely foreign and so exquisitely graceful in habit and so palm-like in their appearance, that a group of these alone of say ten or twelve planted on raised ground cannot fail to give a pleasing effect. And if we add to the Dracaena, Hardy Palms, Boronias, Aralias, Tree Ferns, Acanthus, Paulownias, Ailanthus and a few such like plants, we at once transform this portion of the garden and will name it the "Sub Tropical".

Horticulture was entering an enormously exciting and explosive era, with rare new shrubs from Chile, south-west China, New Zealand and Australia becoming available. Once propagated, these were being incorporated into many of the gardens designed by Treseders'. Unfortunately, the records of the majority of these commissions have been lost, but the beautiful gardens that survive in Cornwall and south Devon are testimony to John's ingenuity and expertise.[12]

St Just-in-Roseland nurseries

Soon after his return to Truro, John began to search for a more favourable, sheltered site, independent of a private garden, in which he could grow stocks of subtropical ornamental plants, especially palms and other new introductions, without protection. He was fortunate to discover such a site adjoining the picturesque and sheltered churchyard of St Just-in-Roseland, which he was able to lease from the rector, the Revd Humfrey Davis, who was also interested in horticulture. To his delight, John found that all kinds of tender plants flourished in the sheltered, humid atmosphere; and, as a bonus, the creation of this nursery greatly assisted Treseders' in the provision of their specialities to the St Mawes area, since the distance by road from Truro to St Mawes, skirting all the rivers, was tiresomely long. John and his family were very fond of this nursery, and his wife's diaries reveal that they all spent many month-long holidays at St Just-in-Roseland, enjoying their wonderful plants and the warm climate. An old Treseders' catalogue shows a photograph of the St Just-in-Roseland nursery, packed full of John's exotic plants.

This excellent acquisition coincided with plans to extend the railway, by way of a new branch line from St Austell to St Just-in-Roseland, in order to service a proposed extension to Falmouth Docks on the Roseland side of the River Fal. St Mawes was also becoming very popular as a resort, and the more wealthy Edwardians were building many new houses in the town. However, the dock developments were delayed by the First World War, and, after almost a quarter of a century of business, Treseders' branch nursery at St Just-in-Roseland was given up in the mid-1920s, although it was subsequently maintained for many years by their ex-foreman, Frank Collins. Fortunately, the proposed dock never materialized, so this side of the River Fal has remained stunningly beautiful and relatively unspoilt by development. The graveyard has long since expanded, using the spaces among many of John Treseder's original specimen plants: *Trachycarpus fortunei*, *Gunnera manicata*, *Drimys winteri*, pittosporum and bamboo still flourish in its superb microclimate. It remains as a living reminder of his venture, and its beauty, serenity and tranquillity prompted the poet laureate, John Betjeman, to comment that St-Just-in-Roseland churchyard was 'to many people the most beautiful churchyard on earth.'[13] John's granddaughter, Marie Louise Treseder, Neil's elder sister, should have the last word though. She started work at the office of the Truro nursery when she was 12 years old, and records childhood days at St Just-in-Roseland in her memoirs:

> As children we were taken there in the horse and trap via King
> Harry Ferry and we had to walk up most of the hills to save the
> horse. When we reached the Nursery at St Just we loved it. Pasties
> were taken for a picnic and the kettle boiled over a smoky fire.
> The smell there was quite unique – the Mexican Incense Plant
> – Eupatorum of which there were large bushes. We could stand
> underneath the giant Tree Ferns. We looked forward to the times
> when the Figs and Medlars were ripe and there was also a delicious
> Box Apple tree. At the Church end of this Nursery was a small,
> furnished cottage in which my Aunt Anne Treseder stayed for
> weekends from time to time ...

Eucalyptus beauchampiana

In Australia, eucalyptus had been a feature of the woodland environment, and John Garland Treseder was so impressed by their fast growth, comparative hardiness and evergreen habit, with leaf colours ranging from blues to greys, to silver, and powdery whites, that by 1904 his nursery stocked almost 40 different varieties. His favourite was his own introduction, *Eucalyptus beauchampiana*. One of the earliest references to *Eucalyptus beauchampiana* is in a letter John wrote to Augustus Bowler, of Riddeton House in Hertfordshsire, in 1903:

> We introduced this beautiful hardy variety ourselves from a re-mote district in Australia and [in] our trials with many others E. Beauchampiana has proved itself to stand from 16–20° of frost without the least injury.
>
> We believe it would thrive with you. We have E. Globulus with stem 4" [10 cm] through, killed one night and alongside a young plant with tender growth of E. Beauchampiana escaping uninjured – on introducing this new variety the writer sent it to the best Authorities for identification and could not find anywhere that the sort was known and therefore he named it after his wife's maiden name 'Beauchamp'. We have in pots limited stock of plants 3–4ft height @ 30/- per dozen.

After a number of years cultivation and careful checking of the records of eucalyptus introductions, John was unable to find a similar speci-men, so he wrote to the Royal Horticultural Society on 19 March 1906, to promote the plant:

> We have pleasure in enclosing 3/- balance of our subscription and beg to bring before your kind notice a <u>new hardy Eucalyptus</u> which we have introduced from Australia as there was not one of the kind sent over before – we have named it Eucalyptus Beau-champiana – we have done this after sending it to the best authori-ties [I] should say that they have never seen the variety before, it is quite distinct and being quite hardy, we think should become a commercial favourite with all planters – one senior partner spent 29 years in Australia and being always on the look out for good hardy trees and plants has at least found this which we believe will prove a valuable introduction – can you assist us in making it pop-ular? Perhaps you will kindly advise us as to the best way to favour. We may mention that it has stood here 20 degrees of frost without the least injury – the shoots have been quite frozen in the pots. The plants have been left open without plunging in the soil – our

trials now extend over three years. We are sending you a branch by
this post and should much like to hear from you on the subject.

The 'Gardeners Chronicle' figured it some months ago.

The previous year, in July 1905, the *Gardeners' Chronicle* had issued the
following feature, in an attempt to identify the species:

'The Beauchamp Eucalyptus' (?=E. Cinerea, F.v.M.)

… This species is not included in Muller's *Eucalyptographia*, but
finds a place in Bentham's *Flora Australiensis, iii, 239*. Mr Worthing-
ton Smith's drawing sufficiently indicates the appearance of the
specimen, so that we need only add that the wiry branchlets are
purplish in colour; the leaves, some alternate, others opposite, are
glaucous and studded with glands on both surfaces and that the
veins are purplish in colour. E. cinerea is a native of New South
Wales. The tree may be called in gardens the Beauchamp Eucalyptus, but care should be taken not to create confusion by using a
Latin name until the identity of the species is rendered certain…
We do not know whether the species is included in the rich collection of the late Mr Rashleigh at Menabilly…

(This last remark is particularly interesting because John Treseder was
regularly sending specimen trees and shrubs to Mr Rashleigh at Menabilly by train, to be collected from Par station.) There then followed
considerable research and debate in various horticultural publications
concerning the true species,[14] but it was not until 1930 that John's eucalyptus was identified in Edgar Thurston's *British & Foreign Trees and
Shrubs in Cornwall. Eucalyptus beauchampiana* was later identified with *E.
stuartiana*, now known as *E. bridgesiana*.

Garden style

John Garland Treseder possessed a great gift – a knowledge of horticulture which grew from handling the plants he loved. Although his
landscaping skills may have come from his apprenticeship with Edward Kemp, it was his untutored lifetime's experience with Australasian
plants that was to put him in such high regard throughout the horticultural world. A typical Treseder garden of John's designing, in the period
1896–1914, would have included *Pinus radiata* and *Cupressus macrocarpa*
to provide the wind protection that was so necessary for the successful
planting of more tender plants. His landscape designs loosely incorpo-

rated ideas from Kemp, but made good use of his own more natural style, achieved by establishing different levels within the gardens and creating a cross-over of both traditional and new ideas with his favoured tree fern grotto, groups of dracaena (*Cordyline australis*), eucalyptus, hydrangea, flowering cherry, rhododendron and roses.

John Garland Treseder died in 1923 at the age of 82 years, continuing his involvement with horticulture right up to the day of his death. He is buried in the Society of Friends Quaker churchyard in Truro, alongside his wife, Mary.

Notes

1   This fast American tea clipper was built in 1851, length 235 ft [72 m], main mast 200 ft [61 m], weight 1,783 tons [1,617 tonnes]. She became water-soaked, and by 1862 her passages were much slower. She was sold to James Baines of Liverpool who used her for the Queensland emigrant trade, carrying around 400 emigrants. See Bazil Lubbock & Jack Spurling, *The Best of Sail*, 1972.

2   The International Camellia Society, *The International Camellia Register*, 1993, Vol. 2, p. 1844: 'Thomas Treseder, *c. japonica*. Hazelwood's Nursery Catalogue 1949, p.13. Crimson, veined darker and striped white. Medium large, formal double. Originated in the old Treseder Nursery (Sydney) and released by Hazelwood's Nursery, Epping, NSW Australia. Abbreviation Tom Treseder.'

3   G. & S. Jellicoe *et al.*, *The Oxford Companion to Gardens*, 1986.

4   Taken from J. Visick, *Travelling Trees*, 2004.

5   For a list of plants exported to Bosahan from Australia in July 1890, see Appendix 1.

6   These are the original botanical names used by John Garland Treseder in 1911.

7   For a list of seeds and plants exported from Australia in the years 1890–93, see Appendix 2.

8   For a list of plants exported to Tasmania for Hobart Public Gardens, see Appendix 3.

9   Praed at Trevethoe, near Lelant, is recorded in Fraser's survey of *c.* 1780 as having discovered the effectiveness of *Pinus radiata*, the example being followed by such tree planters as the Bassetts of Tehidy and the Rashleighs.

10 A similar method is used today in Holland, where nurseries grow con-

siderable numbers of trees to mature sizes for replanting to give 'instant' impact.

11 For a list of early Australasian plant introductions (*c.* 1904), see Appendix 5.

12 Treseders' Nursery landscaped public parks and gardens in Truro, Helston, Camborne, Redruth, Newquay, St Ives, and Saltash, as well as the grounds of Truro cathedral, Lis Escop (the Bishop's old palace), the Convent of the Epiphany (now the Alverton Manor Hotel), and numerous vicarage gardens. Those large gardens in which Treseders were involved, and which I have been able to identify from records are Bochym, Boconnoc, Doydon, Glendurgan, Heligan, Menabilly, Nansidwell, Penrose, Place (Fowey), Trebah, Tregothnan, Trengwainton, Trewithen, Treloyhan, Tregenna, Willapark, and Higher Faughan, the home of the Newlyn artist Stanhope Forbes. In the early 1900s, Treseders' clients included Sir Lewis Molesworth of Trewarthenick; Dr Harden of St Mawes; Mr Whitley of Penarth, Truro; Revd Tyringham of Trevethoe, and Captain Penberthy of Lelant; Mr John Roberts of the Lizard, and Countess Marie Borst of St Columb Minor. In 1897 John wrote to Mr Backhouse, MP, at Trebah, suggesting improvements in the landscaping and grouping of plants to create a more interesting environment. Sadly, pages of this letter are very brittle and rather damaged, making the list of plants difficult to decipher.

13 *Cornwall: A Shell Guide*, 1964.

14 See, for example, the *Gardeners' Chronicle*, 17 March 1906, p. 6.

3 Ira Garland Treseder, 1877–1967

Introduction

Ira Garland Treseder was the seventh child in the family of eleven children (five boys and six girls) of John Garland and Mary Treseder. He was born in 1877 at Parramatta in Australia, shortly after his parents had returned to that country after a period of nine years working in the family nursery business at Moresk in Truro. When they were in their very early teens, Ira and his brothers Charles, Sidney and Jack all worked with their father in his nurseries in Sydney. Vast numbers of Burrawang Palms (*Macrozamia spiralis*) grew in the bush nearby, and, prompted by a chance letter of enquiry from a French seed house, their father wondered if there might be a market for the fronds of these lovely plants in the florist trade. Ira was therefore given the job of sending sample fronds to the Treseders' international contacts. In later years, he wrote about the experience and the method he used to prepare the fronds for export:

> The palm fronds were cut to full length, tied in bundles of ten and passed through tanks of boiling water to toughen them, hung up to dry and then sent to the nursery's packing department at Ashfield to be placed in large cases which were well battened down to keep them flat and firm. In the course of time orders were received from France, America, England and Germany and over a period of six months over 100,000 palm fronds were exported to Hamburg alone.

In the period 1890–95, Ira travelled widely in the untamed Australian bush, collecting vast quantities of eucalyptus and palm seeds. In the main, these were intended for Treseders' now considerable international export trade, but some were germinated at their own nursery for planting in the grand gardens and government parks which his father had been commissioned to design and plant in and around Sydney.

Not long after their parents had left Australia to return to Cornwall once again in 1896, Ira and his brother Jack were also encouraged to emigrate to England: John had cabled them to say that his business in Truro was flourishing. The two brothers gradually wound up their father's Australian nurseries and other business ventures. Shortly before leaving, Ira married an 'Australian-born girl' called Mary Grieve, and the newlyweds travelled to England on the P & O steamship *Medic* for their honeymoon. Ira and Mary rented

Ira Garland Treseder.

one of John's houses in Paul's Row in Truro, and when Jack and his wife arrived in Truro they were to live in Daniell Road.[1] Most of their brothers and sisters had already married and remained settled in Australia – one brother became an artesian well-borer, and claimed to have drilled the deepest borehole in Australia.

Prior to the advent of the motorcar, few visitors were able to enjoy the extraordinary grounds of the family nursery: most plants ordered from the nursery were sent to the customers by train. In those early days, Ira had the job of transporting the large packages to the railway station in Truro by donkey cart. Every time he reached the bottom of Richmond Hill, which leads up to the station, his donkey would try to lie down and refused to go any further, making this frequent journey an embarrassing and detested task. As Treseders' acquired more trained gardening staff, in order to expand the business and increase their reputation, Ira joined his father 'out on the road'. Each frequently travelled, independently, throughout the south-west, from Bristol into Wales, and across to Bournemouth and Torquay, calling on town councils, hoteliers, builders and home-owners, encouraging them to have their grounds and gardens professionally designed and planted. Ira's mother, Mary, kept a diary, and her entries at this time show that the two men were seldom at home: the nursery was attended to by Ira's brother Jack and sister Annie, while their flower and seed shop in Truro was run by another sister, Hannah. During this period came the birth of Interflora, 'The Flowers by Wire Organisation'.[2] To facilitate this new style of floristry and improve contact between the nurseries and their flower shop, the Treseders were among the first in Truro to install a telephone – their number was Truro 26. Treseders' Nurseries had become an important local family business.

A few years earlier, Ira's father had been given a horticultural book which, from its well-worn condition, was obviously referred to regularly. Its contents were to influence the development of their Cornish business for many years to come, resulting in Treseders' Nurseries becoming the most respected and successful horticultural nursery in the south-west of England. The title-page of this great tome reads

The Rural Improver

or, a

Practical Treatise,

on the

Nature and Management of Such Rural

Scenes and Objects,

as are necessary to promote the

Comfort, Convenience, and Embellishment

of the residences of

the Higher Ranks of Society.

The whole founded on experience, and deduced from well-known natural principles, which are immutable.

By W. PONTEY;

Author of The Profitable Planter, and Forest Pruner

The Ponteys, together with the Veitches, were prominent nurserymen in Devon. In 1827, some 70 years previously, this volume had belonged to the well-known and widely respected James Mitchinson, who had been head gardener for the Pendarves estate near Camborne. His son, on his own retirement from horticulture in 1899, gave it to 'his father's dear old friend John Garland Treseder'. James Mitchinson was a reputable member of the Royal Horticultural Society of Cornwall, and responsible for an important collection of indigenous plants in the Redruth area. Botany had become not just a popular but an extremely serious hobby, and Cornwall was acclaimed for valuable documents recording the county's enormous diversity of unusual and rare wild plant species.

The purpose of Pontey's marvellous book was to explain how to create sympathetic designs for parkland and country estates. The planting was to be carried out in such a way that every tree and under-planted shrub should 'be considered for their shade, shelter, usefulness as a place for retirement and variety.' Throughout, the emphasis is upon the visual enjoyment made possible by the grouping together of different plants, with careful consideration always being given to the garden's long-term development. In a chapter entitled 'Of a Flower Garden', the author remarks that

> Considering the amusements of the female part of our species,
> to be naturally bounded within much narrower limits than the
> male, it seems only equitable, that they should be provided with so
> much greater variety of such objects, as will afford them sources
> of grateful, elegant and healthful recreation at all seasons when it
> is proper for them to taste the air in all its native sweetness and pu-
> rity. A walkway should be so broad as that two ladies walking arm
> in arm might find it perfectly commodious to be enjoyed.

(The practical advice on how to prune shrubs seems rather mundane in comparison!) Ira Treseder's skill was to incorporate many of the features from this gardening book into his own plans and designs for the modern, greatly reduced scale of gardens belonging to his expanding list of new customers.

When Ira and Jack were made directors of the family business trading as Treseder & Co., their nursery letter paper became more flamboyant, using attractively coloured illustrations advertising the new fertilizers they were using and selling, and *Dracaena tresederiana*.

In May 1903, with their business expanding so rapidly, Treseders' employed a professional gardener, Charles B. Ussher, who, it appears, trained at Kew. He undertook the duties of nursery foreman, and was especially responsible for everything under glass, starting on a salary of 25 shillings per week, to be increased in relation to the value of his work. By now their own nursery stock was being propagated in house, especially the palms and phormiums that were becoming so popular with their clients. In 1905 Ira wrote to numerous nurseries throughout Britain and the continent, promoting the nursery's stock of 3,000 phormiums and 4,000 cordylines, and listing almost three dozen varieties of eucalyptus.[3] New varieties of plants were constantly being acquired: plant hunters brought home an increasing variety of new discoveries from around the world, and Treseder & Co. also propagated many plants from cuttings and seeds taken from the many rare shrubs growing on the private estates throughout the county.

One of Ira's first and most important commercial contracts, in 1910, was to construct a garden in the grounds of the newly built Fishguard Hotel in Wales, owned by the Great Western Railway Company. This involved extensive landscaping of the woodland slopes, and led to many more large contracts in that area, both private and public. Treseders' catalogue of 1913 included an article about the commission as an advertisement for the garden design aspect of the business:

> We had the honour of creating the Fishguard Gardens for the
> GWR Co beginning in March, 1910, and continuing the work
> of laying out and planting until the end of May. We were able to
> select the position for each Shrub and Tree, and also for the Rock-
> gardens and Alpine Plants planted therein. A little natural dell
> favoured our making the most of; and here we were able to plant
> Tree Ferns, Bamboos, Gunneras, hardy Palms etc., and, taking to
> their new home, these sub-tropical plants seem to revel. A little at-
> tention helped them to establish themselves. For the Rock-garden
> we were able to get weather-worn rocks hard by, of which we used
> 100 tons. We took advantage of the wood, and its grateful shade,
> to arrange our walks, so that they measure in all some three-quar-
> ters of a mile. Where the shade was found to be too dark we were
> able to carefully cut some branches to let in light and sunshine. We
> planted in the woods numbers of Hydrangeas, and, where not too
> shady, Rhododendrons. In all were planted shrubs representing
> eighteen countries, and, having a knowledge of the native habitat
> of a great many, selected the very place we knew they would take
> to, and so, with careful study, nearly all the plants have done well.
> Fruit-gardens were also in our list of work, in which we intro-
> duced Trees in many forms, such as Cordons – horizontal and
> oblique, as well as Espaliers, Bushes, and Pyramids. The better
> kinds of Gooseberry and Currants came in for a share of atten-
> tion, as well as Strawberries, Raspberries, and Loganberries, etc.
> The Great Western Railway Company for whom we carried out

this contract, took a keen interest, having large interests here, and wishing to prove what the climate will produce. Our sub-tropical effects in the grounds were produced by planting two hundred and fifty Dracaenas, many hardy Palms, Phormiums, Bamboos, etc.

In April 1912, Jack decided to break away from the family business in Truro to open an independent landscape gardening business at Clapham Park, London. Treseder & Co. had already established numerous connections in this area, and Jack realized that there were wider opportunities in the fast-expanding capital. He had no nursery as such, but for many years his conspicuous corner-site at Raleigh Lodge, Brixton Hill, was a local landmark, subtropical plants such as cordylines and the Chusan palm, *Trachycarpus fortunei*, not having been seen there before. He employed a considerable staff on garden construction and landscaping contracts, and, according to family memoirs, was responsible for numerous important assignments in the London area.

Gradually, as his father took on more of a consultancy role, Ira rose to the challenge of promoting through his catalogues the increasing numbers of new introductions that had acclimatized so well in the sheltered gardens of the south-west. The First World War interrupted his horticultural career, and Ira joined the army. Fortunately, he survived the war, his father (then in his late 70s) keeping the nursery business ticking over with the help of Ira's sister, Annie. With the end of the war there was a rapid expansion in house-building, as more people were able to buy their own homes instead of renting. Ira was once again travelling around the West Country and along the south coast of England, securing landscaping contracts and persuading these new homeowners that they could enhance their gardens with the vast range of new, rare plants that were rapidly becoming available through his contacts worldwide. Treseder & Co. now employed a staff of 26 people, and although he was concentrating on garden and park design, Ira secured extensive contracts with the Great Western Railway, planting woodlands along the scarred embankments, and landscaping many of the main- and branch-line stations throughout Cornwall, Wales, and south Devon.

It is difficult to imagine the excitement the Treseder men and their staff must have experienced on receiving shipments of new and strange plant introductions. Obviously, the new species could not be sold to customers without having been given a careful 'trial run' at the Moresk nurseries, favoured with the long Cornish growing periods and mild winters. Along with the experience of propagating the Australasian stock, supplied to nurseries throughout Britain and Europe, Ira was able to gain detailed practical knowledge of the cultivation of exotic species – their tolerances, habits, and flowering periods. It was information that took time to acquire, reliable observations being possible only after several years of careful nurturing to allow the specimens to settle down to seasonal changes, vagaries of the weather, and the Truro soil.

Carnivals

As a means of local advertising, Ira, with the assistance of his staff, regularly entered the Truro carnival. Each year a spectacular float was designed by his driver, Bertie Carveth, and the nursery delivery lorry was decorated with vast quantities of hydrangea blooms from the St Just-in-Roseland nurseries. The carnival was a great social event, and the preparation of the float was entered into with enthusiasm. One year Bertie designed an enormous peacock called the 'Hoodlum Bird'; another year an aeroplane, with his eldest son, Kenneth, dressed as the pilot, representing the Aeronautical Schneider Trophy;[4] then a railway steam engine, and many others. These extravagant and ambitious displays invariably won numerous awards and silver cups.

Kenneth Carveth and the Aeronautical Schneider Trophy on Treseders' carnival float, 1932.

Treseders' nursery catalogues

For generations, Treseders' Nurseries' catalogues have been an invaluable guide to both horticultural trainees and commercial establishments involved in horticulture. The oldest catalogues in my possession date from the early 1900s. A great many plant names have been changed over the years since the original introductions, and some are no longer available commercially; but even today, with the plethora of gardening books, and television and radio programmes, Treseders' catalogues are still used as a reliable reference point by both professional and amateur gardeners, because of the wealth of technical and horticultural information they contain. Indeed, I have heard several horticulturists describe them as 'gardening bibles'.

Catalogue cover, c. 1900.

Ira Garland Treseder's original nursery catalogues are classics in themselves. The very early Treseder & Co. catalogues promoted their favoured Australasian introductions, and subsequent editions reveal a steady increase in the variety of plant species available. These are clearly catalogues written by a man who loved and understood the rare new plants he nurtured, and express his expert knowledge and personal experience of how well each particular species had acclimatized to the Cornish environment. Very often, Ira was the first nurseryman to write a complete description of the habit and tolerance of exotic plants, and his personal copies of catalogues from the early 1900s are full of pencilled notes and amendments, each careful and detailed description being meticulously refined. He was continuously seeking to encourage his customers to improve their gardens with the rapidly increasing variety of interesting plant species becoming available, and, by 1911, claimed that his nurseries sold plants from over 40 countries.[5] Regions of origin given alongside the names of new introductions include the Sierra Nevada in California, Mexico, Japan, New Zealand, Australia, Tasmania, India, Kashmir, Nepal, the Himalayas, China, Chile, Patagonia, Valdivia

(Brazil), the Organ Mountains (Chile), Montevideo, Ireland, the Crimea, Afghanistan, Spain, Portugal, Minorca, Tenerife, Lebanon, and the Cape of Good Hope. The international door to horticulture was opening wide. At the bottom of each page there was a pithy tag for the reader: 'Any of the Fir Tribe not mentioned here can be supplied'; 'Rare Australian and New Zealand plants a speciality'; 'We have a fine show of beautiful Tree Ferns'; and 'Our slogan – plant more trees.'[6]

As his business became more sophisticated, Ira also sold horticultural accoutrements, from pots and labels to fertilizers, and his catalogues informed customers of the numerous additional services that his nurseries provided, such as the hire of pot plants for functions, and garden and landscape design, alongside lists of seeds, vegetables, trees and shrubs, bedding plants and climbers for sale. Illustrations in the earliest Treseders' catalogues include etchings of roses and large houses with vine-covered walls, and photographs of views around their subtropical nursery grounds, both at Truro and St Just-in-Roseland, proudly portraying the Treseders' lush Australasian introductions, together with the now ubiquitous giant tree ferns. Later, in order to promote his landscaping skills, Ira replaced these with photographs of newly laid rockeries, and the landscaping of the grounds at the Fishguard Hotel.

Ira was continually reaching out to a wider clientele: many potential new clients had only small gardens, so he took care to introduce his readers to his plants' suitability for various types of small garden, with sections devoted to cottage, flower, rock, town, and 'window gardening', alongside those which discussed 'Plants by the sea', ponds, and woodlands. There were also numerous articles on horticultural subjects in which the Treseder men had specialized and become famous. The following example is taken from a catalogue of *c.* 1913:

Sub Tropical Effects in the Garden

Cornwall and Devonshire enjoy a climate unequalled anywhere, for what is called in gardening "sub-tropical effects". There are doubtless many sheltered nooks and corners in other counties in England and Wales; if so, they should be taken advantage of. Where position favours, a group of the following will be sure to give satisfaction as a tropical scene. Having detected your sheltered corner, raise the ground at least 4 feet [1.2 m] and have some real good weather-worn rocks of a large size placed naturally, then

plant three Tree Ferns in a group among the rocks and three
Ailanthus altissima, 1 *Gunnera manicata*, 3 *Aralia spinosa*, 3 *Chamaerops
humilis*, 1 *Trachycarpus fortunei*, 1 *Eulalia japonica*, 5 *Cordyline australis*,
3 Bamboos (graceful sorts), 12 Japan lilies in variety and cover the
surface of the soil with a carpet of *Soleirolia* (*urticaceae*) so that your
plants and rocks will rise from a carpeted bank. The foreground
should be a close shorn lawn. This group, in our judgement, will
dignify any garden and will increase in beauty as the years go by.
Other large leaved shrubs may be added if it is wished to extend
the group but be sure to do the work with great care.

After the First World War, communications improved and Cornwall
was promoted as a holiday resort. Coastal properties therefore became
increasingly fashionable, resulting in a growing market for plants that
could survive the conditions of maritime gardens. With his specialist
knowledge and business interests, Ira was at the forefront in explaining
the benefits of, and encouraging the fashion for, seaside gardens, as his
1924 catalogue shows:

Sea-side Gardens

The sea coast of England and Wales is really so beautiful, that we
do not wonder at the fact that the best people, from choice, are
building houses and taking up their residence near the sea – but, as
someone has said: "When men grow intelligently, they may build
stately, but certainly will garden finely". The question comes: How
shall we counteract the bleak winds? We know if we have shelter
we can grow most of the beautiful varieties of plants and shrubs
seen in the wide world – but how can we get up the shelter, and
what shall we plant for this shelter? is the great question.

  Now these groups should have curved outlines, and be arranged in such a way they will look as picturesque as possible, not
only from the house, but from the sea, and, if formed properly,
will have a most charming effect. The groups should be of various sizes and shapes, to give variety – but all with curved outlines.
Now, the land for planting should be trenched 18 inches [46 cm]
deep, and planted in the following way: outside, nearest the sea,
furze, double and single; atriplex, veronica, heath in variety: Tama-
risk in variety, broom white and yellow; olearia and phormium;
these should be mixed along the outline. The next planting will be

euonymus, escallonia, sycamore and Cornish elms. The next inside should be *Pinus pinaster*, *Pinus radiata*, *Cupressus macrocarpa*, *Pinus nigra* subsp. *laricio*. Then you may plant laurestinus, birch, beech, English elms, evergreen oak, alder, elder (golden), elder (silver), elder (fern-leaved). Inside this plantation you may put in elaeagnus, in variety; coronilla; cistus in variety; veronica in variety and cordyline. The outside of each group will be sheltered by hurdles, in which will intertwine furze. This temporary shelter will remain for two years, when it will be found that the Trees and Shrubs will be well established. All planting must be done thickly – not more than 4 feet [1.2 m] apart being allowed, and even less than this on the windy side.

After this is done for shelter, we advise mounds of a natural formation to be thrown up, the top of these mounds turfed, and even slope inwards, for the first 3 feet [1 m]. Then you can begin planting shrubs of the more tender kinds on the inner slope – of course care must be taken that drainage be secured. The sunk garden can then be formed in whatever design agreed upon. There will not be space here to go into full details of the seaside garden, but we think we have said enough, perhaps to give the reader an idea of the successful way. You may have your rock garden here, in which will be placed not only rare alpine plants, but native rock plants which you may collect on the coast.

In all cases, when selecting for sea-side gardens, care must be taken to plant only those kinds which love the sea air – in flowering plants, carnations, pinks, dianthus, statice, helianthemums, alyssum, anemone, arabis, campanulas, lychnis, narcissus, poppy, veronica, centaurea, crocosmia, tradescantia, heleniums, gaillardia, and any plant with silver foliage.

Gardening contracts took the firm all over the south-west, and further afield. Treseder & Co.'s landscaping staff had become so busy that, for contracts at long distances from the nursery, the property owners were invariably required to find their own jobbing labour, with Ira or his foreman acting only on a consultancy basis.

Throughout the early twentieth century, there was an overwhelming appetite for 'acclimatized exotics', a taste which the Treseders were ever ready to feed. In the 1924 catalogue, Ira gave advice to those beginning to replant their gardens in a period of renewed economic prosperity:

Rare Shrubs

Rare shrubs, which may be planted in Cornish and Devonshire gardens, and most places near the south coast, are so desirable, and at present so much sought after, that a word of two about them may not be out of place. Most of these beautiful shrubs are indigenous to dry countries, and yet many of them seem to thrive better in favoured spots than in their native home.

Our experience in travel has helped us in the culture of these valuable additions to the garden.

As many of them grow on the coast of New Zealand, Australia, and Tasmania, fully exposed to the bleak winds, they will be found quite at home on our coast. Nearly all do best where the soil is thoroughly drained, and, indeed, inclined to be dry, while many love a sheltered nook. Three months without rain is not unusual in their native country. Yet they can be educated to take the moisture of this country, if provision is made to take the water off quickly from their roots. A dry bank is favourable, but never a very wet piece of land. To attempt to speak of the beauty of these handsome shrubs is to fail, for no description can give them their due. They are not only rare in their introduction, but rare in their colours, in their leaves and flowers, and rare in their habits of growth. Many of them exude perfume, exquisite in the extreme. It seems to us, where possible, a few of these, at least, should be planted in the garden.

If our customers will give us the position of their land, we will advise them where and what to plant, and, in improving the garden, it will be found necessary to move all unsightly and even common shrubs to make room for the better-class varieties.

Special mention may be made of the Acacias (mimosa) in their many kinds. In various parts of Cornwall these shrubs may be grown for profit i.e. for cut flowers. In our judgement, our own climate is quite equal to the South of France, where the blossom of mimosa is produced in such abundance.

All the olearias, for the most part, are natives of New Zealand. It is well known that the phormium, in different varieties, thrive on our coast, as well as the cordylines and are even used for shelter. Both of these are New Zealand natives. The *Brachyglottis repanda* is also a very beautiful New Zealand shrub. The *Calamagrostis arundi-*

nacea is a grass-like plant, with drooping plumes, 3 feet [1 m] long, which when cut, and placed in vases, keep a long time and are very pretty for ornamentation. The pittosporums are worthy of special mention, for they are amongst the chief of New Zealand shrubs.

In speaking of Australian shrubs, we would suggest planting the callistemon (Bottlebrush), correas, myrtus, grevilleas, myoporums, and ozothamnus, etc. etc. We feel it only wants a little acquaintance with the many beautiful Australian shrubs mentioned in this catalogue, to so popularise them, as to suggest the introduction of an Australian quarter in the garden.

Spain, India, China, South America, Brazil and California, have given us many choice shrubs of late years, which have flourished well in Cornwall and South Devon, and when judiciously introduced amongst the Australian and New Zealand shrubs, have proved very successful in making the garden exceptionally picturesque.

When we have mentioned Japan and Mexico, from which we have drawn so many treasures, it may be said we have ransacked the world to enrich our English gardens.

As the demand for garden layouts increased outside Cornwall, Ira opened a small branch nursery at Plymouth. This was later transferred to Paignton, both for the retail of nursery stock and as headquarters for garden contracts throughout south Devon. He had, by this time, designed large and wonderful gardens in Surrey, Kent, Kingswear (Coleton Fishacre), Salcombe, Teignmouth and Torquay, for many of which written records still survive.

As the business expanded, Ira had a beautiful colonial-style bungalow built at the entrance to the nurseries, which he called 'Illawarra', the name of one of the places in Australia he had visited as a boy. Here, he and his wife, Mary, raised their young family, Marie (Mary) and the twins, Neil and Isabelle, while the nursery manager, Mr Barnes, and his family moved into their old cottage in the middle of the nurseries, taking care of the boilers for the heated greenhouses, watering the plants, and opening the cold frames at weekends. The twin brothers Jim and Jack Lilly also trained at the nurseries. Jack married one of Mr Barnes' daughters, and was later to become head gardener at Trelissick, Feock, near King Harry Ferry.[7] By now, Ira and his sister Annie had been joined in the family business by his eldest daughter, Mary, and son, Neil. Neil's twin sister, Isabelle, looked after their Truro city-centre flower shop at 4 Cathedral Lane.

Unfortunately, Second World War restrictions on staff and transport forced the closure of the Paignton depot. When Miss Annie retired from the partnership in 1950, a limited company was formed under the title of Treseders' Nurseries (Truro) Ltd., with Ira, Neil and Mary as directors. After the death of his wife Mary, Ira married Mabel Chapple from Penberth in west Cornwall, a prominent figure in the Women's Institute movement, and on retiring in 1955, he passed over the control of the family nurseries to Neil and Mary.

Plant introductions

Family documents show that, during his career, Ira received recognition from the Royal Horticultural Society for two plant introductions. He was awarded the RHS Award of Garden Merit in November 1938 for his re-introduction of *Cosmos atrosanguineus* (*Bidens atrosanguinea*), an old Victorian plant that had gone out of fashion. He had exhibited this rare, black-flowering genus in London earlier that year, describing it as 'a beautiful herbaceous tuberous-rooted plant, bearing profusions of dark chocolate-red, coreopsis-like flowers, on wiry stalks which smell remarkably of cocoa. These flowers last well when cut and show up best against a background of white gypsophila.' Ira's other introduction was *Populus candicans* 'Aurora', for which he was proud to receive the RHS Award of Garden Merit in 1954. In later years, Neil described in an undated paper how this was discovered:

> In 1954 our remarkable pink and cream variegated form of the Ontario Poplar (*Populus candicans* 'Aurora') received an Award of Merit when shown at one of the Royal Horticultural Society's fortnightly shows in London. In the late 1920s my father, Ira Garland Treseder came across a variegated sport on a tree of the Ontario Poplar, *Populus candicans*, which was growing in a North Devon garden. It was autumn, and apart from streaks of white on some of the leaves, it did not then reveal its full potential. The cutting rooted and grew into an attractive tree but its full value as a garden ornamental was not appreciated for a long time because of the Second World War.
>
> The early leaves are light green just like those of most other poplars and it is not until June that young shoots appear with

leaves shaded pink and cream, the effect of the coloured leaves of this tree is conspicuous from a considerable distance and is more showy over a longer period than the Dove Tree (*Davidia*). Just imagine the complaints we used to receive from disappointed garden owners. Our stock reply was, 'Please write to us again when the tree begins to grow.' We never heard from them again.

Because of the leaf colourings I decided to name it 'Aurora' after the goddess of dawn and, in July 1954, we sent cut material to a Royal Horticultural Society's show. In spite of widespread prejudice against variegated plants at that time it was given an Award of Garden Merit as a hardy ornamental leaved tree. I noticed that trees which had been robbed of the young side shoots for propagation purposes in autumn produced coloured foliage as soon as growth commenced in May and realised that the display period could be extended by spur pruning in winter.

Garden style

The gardens designed by Ira during his landscaping career (1909–45) were generally constructed on virgin sites, and were much smaller than those owned by the Cornish gentry with which his father had been involved. He developed a unique knowledge of maritime planting, and would always consider the visual aspect from both within and without his gardens, particularly when a seaside property could be viewed from the water. He realized the value of grouping plants to create more of an impact, and of instructing his clients' gardeners on the future maintenance of more unusual species. He invariably incorporated a pond, laying down networks of underground pipes for the circulation of the water, and surrounded it with bamboos, gunnera, and many of the new water-loving plants being brought into the country by the plant hunters. The introduction of attractive rust-grey St Issey slate in the style of crazy paving became fairly prominent and fashionable, as did the addition of a rockery. Suitable granite rocks were obtained from the numerous local quarries, and the soil around the rockery site was raised, enabling it to be sufficiently drained to accommodate the ever-increasing selection of compact alpine novelties – a strategy he had employed during the landscaping work at the Fishguard Hotel in Wales.

Retracing Australian roots

In 1953, some 50 years after emigrating from Australia, Ira, now in his mid-70s, returned there to trace the family's nurseries. A letter home to Cornwall reports the changes he noticed, and the discoveries he made during the course of his research:

A little over sixty years ago when I was a lad, my father who had a nursery garden at Ashfield, took me to Woy Woy to explore the bush for Burrawang Palms. We did not need to go very far to find them. In the course of time my father purchased a property between Davis Town and MacMasters Beach. His idea was to use the virgin soil for the growing of citrus fruit, apple and plum trees, Norfolk Island Pines, camellias etc which he succeeded in doing.

Transport was difficult then. A small steamer 'The Midget' used to come from Sydney area once a week and would deliver and collect goods at Merrits Wharf which the government had built mainly for collecting timber. The railway to Woy Woy had not been long opened then, there was a short wooden platform and travellers had to contact the guard before leaving Hawkesbury River Station. To stop the train on the return journey one had to hold up the tin flag arrangement by day, and at night, light the lamp attached to a shed on the platform. While this was being done the mosquitoes had a chance of extracting new blood.

Looking back, one cannot but admire the undaunted spirit of the wonderful workmen who blasted away the rock to make those perpendicular cuttings through solid hard stone (no rock drilling machines or bulldozers then) all done mostly with pick and shovel. Just think of the making of the tunnel seven bricks thick over a mile long (so I have been told) men sleeping in tents with practically no protection from mosquitoes.

The bricks were brought by steamer to Cox's Wharf, a rail track being laid from there to the mouth of the tunnel (hence the name Brick Road, Woy Woy). I had not visited the area for 65 years, what a marvellous change. What was dense forest is now studded with pretty little bungalows.

Last week I had the day of all days. Mr Hazelwood, nurseryman of Epping near Hornsby called for me with his car and took me to see Professor Waterhouse, the great camellia specialist. The professor has a charming Scotch wife who soon had tea and cakes before looking at the 200 camellias all sizes, some are the professor's own seedlings, all very wonderful, now coming into bloom. This place is at Gordon on the North Shore line, not far from Hornsby, the town one passes through on the way to Woy Woy. There is a camellia show there next week and if possible Mabel and I will go to see it.

Prof Waterhouse told me that there was a Treseder Catalogue at Mitchells Library opposite the entrance to Sydney Botanic Gardens. I saw the Secretary on the following day and was able to peruse father's old catalogue 1883, mentioning Underwood and Dobroyd Nurseries. What interested me most was the list of 100 varieties of camellias and above an inset copy of a report of father's nursery activity in the Sydney Morning Herald. They are photographing this for me to take it back with me. Another exciting moment was when (Herb) Charles' son produced a copy of a book father wrote entitled 'The Garden', I am trying to get extracts printed for you all.

Reminiscences

We have now reached a time within the memory of many alive today, and it is perhaps fitting to end this chapter with some reminiscences of contemporaries who knew Ira at the nurseries.

There is a family story that on one occasion before John Garland Treseder visited Norfolk Island, he told his wife that their young son, Ira, was old enough to join the expedition. On reaching Norfolk Island, Ira was left with the local inhabitants in their village, while John went into the forests with his companions and guides to gather seeds. He duly sailed back home to Sydney with his precious cargo of seeds and palms, only to be questioned by Mary as to where Ira was. In his enthusiasm about his seed finds, John had forgotten Ira and left him behind: the next vessel to the island was to be in six months' time! (There is a parallel to this story – my youngest brother, Paul, told me that when he was little, he was also left behind when our father, Neil, took him to Trengwainton, became involved in plant discussions with the Bolithos, and then returned to the Truro nurseries without him. Paul was eventually brought home in the Bolithos' chauffeur-driven car.)

Tom Cocking and his five sons, Willy, Ernie, Tommy, Fred and Aubrey, were all trained under Ira. They were paid five shillings a week, the remainder of their wages being held back to pay for their training. Tom's sons became highly respected, self-employed jobbing gardeners; all except Aubrey, who dedicated his working life to the Treseders. After 50 years' service, the Royal Horticultural Society acknowledged his contribution to horticulture by providing his widow with a pension. Tom and his family lived in the cottage at the entrance to the nurseries, which, after having been derelict for some time, was renovated to become the first home of Ira's grandson, my brother Andrew, and his young bride, Marina, in the mid-1960s.

Another employee was Bryan Badcock, who was able to recall many stories about my grandfather. Bryan started work at Treseders' Nurseries as soon as he left school. Mr Ira was 'a true Boss', he said, not a man to mix with the men. Ira's working attire comprised a hat, a brown, knee-length coat, and gaiters. Wherever he went, he was always accompanied by his adored, and adoring, black spaniels. Although Ira was very fair, staff did not have holidays in those early days, except when it was raining too hard for them to work.

Ira continued to make regular visits to the nurseries from his home with Mabel at Penberth until he was 87 years old. He travelled up to Truro weekly by train, bringing with him material from his garden for David Knuckey to propagate. In those days the carriages had compartments and, during the hour-long journey, Ira would commandeer fellow passengers to help him prepare the cuttings. This activity soon became so popular that passengers would wait to get into the same compartment as Ira in order to join in! On Saturdays, Bryan was chosen from the Truro nursery staff to take the train to Penzance, and then the taxi to Penberth, to work in Ira's garden. Although Bryan enjoyed these expeditions, he stood in awe of 'Mr Ira', a very domineering man who did not suffer fools gladly, and would stand no nonsense.

Ira died at the age of 90, in 1967. Like his father, John, he was involved with the plants he loved right up to the time of his death.

Notes

1 Cornwall has always been a close-knit community, and it is interesting how families frequently interconnect. When I first met my husband, my mother-in-law to be, Cicely (Kernick), who, at the time of writing, is in her late 90s, recalled that when she was a young child her parents lived in Daniell Road, Truro, next door to Ira's brother, Jack Bathurst

Treseder and his family. Her mother would look after Jack's young Australian wife when he was away on business visits to London, and the Kernick and Treseder children played together in their garden where there grew a strange tree with crinkly leaves and black, perfumed flowers (pittosporum).

2   See reference to Fred Treseder, Chapter 1, page 19.

3   For a list of eucalyptus and other unusual plants, see Appendix 4.

4   Archive carnival photograph donated by Geoff Carveth.

5   For a list of rare plant introductions, *c.* 1911, see Appendix 6.

6   For a fuller list of these advertising slogans, see Finis, page 105.

7   In 1955 Trelissick was given to the National Trust. Its present garden was created by the then owners, the Copelands.

4   Neil Garland Treseder, 1913–1996

Introduction

My father, Neil Garland Treseder, and his twin sister, Isabelle, were born in 1913. Neil was Ira's only son, and became the fourth generation of plantsmen trading as Treseders' Nurseries, Truro. Like many Truro boys whose family was in business and had strong Methodist connections, Neil was educated at Truro School, situated high on the hill overlooking the city and the river. On leaving school, he spent about a year working at the nurseries with his father, to raise some money to enable him to further his education, before proceeding to the University College of the South West at Exeter (now Exeter University) in 1931, taking a condensed course in Botany and Horticulture, and completing his National Diploma of Horticulture by correspondence course while he was in charge of his father's new branch nurseries at Mannamead, Plymouth.

With improving road transport, the family business was rapidly expanding into the Torbay area, where the south coast resorts enjoyed a climate similar to that of Cornwall, making possible the opening of another branch nursery, in Paignton. A considerable proportion of the turnover at the new Paignton outlet came from hiring out gardeners at an hourly rate, a service that brought in a regular income. The premises included an adjoining lock-up shop and flat, providing Neil with accommodation. By now he had the luxury of his own car, and was able to travel all over Devon and north and east Cornwall to those towns and villages not serviced by the railway, calling (without invitation) on the owners of large, new gardens and on Parish and Town Councils and their Parks Committees. This was hard graft: selling exotic trees and shrubs required perseverance and dedication, as the extravagance of buying ornamental plants was new territory for most householders. Neil recalled that an order of over £10 was something to be remembered. (In those days the basic agricultural weekly wage was only about thirty shillings (£1.50), and petrol was 1s.1d. (about 5p) a gallon. Nevertheless, he was successful, and secured numerous garden design and planting contracts, the results of which continue to influence the Torbay area today, with the *Cordyline australis* (Dracaena palms) along the sea front, and large specimens of *Cupressus macrocarpa* (Monterey cypress) in the parks. On one occasion, Treseders' had an excessive number of young monkey-puzzles (*Araucaria araucana*). While on a journey to Bude to carry out garden designs and contracts in the sheltered Poughill area, Neil called at numerous houses along the way and managed to sell most of the seedlings. Years later he would chuckle and say that anyone who knew of this could follow his route on that day by seeing which gardens still have these huge trees.

However, the Second World War brought an abrupt end to the Plymouth and Paignton nurseries: many of the workers were called up, and Neil returned to Truro to work at the Moresk Nurseries, where he concentrated on vegetable production, even working during the night in the beam from his car headlights. He and his father, Ira, were commissioned to record wireless lectures on 'Digging for Victory', and to visit village halls and rural communities, advising the locals – mostly women, now that the men of fighting age had joined the services – on how to grow their own vegetables. He was also responsible for supervising Italian prisoners of war working on the outlying farms. After the war, the experience of growing their own vegetables encouraged a new interest among the general public in planting ornamental gardens, so that nurseries became revitalized and busy with an increased trade in plants.

As previously mentioned, by the mid-1950s the original partnership of Treseder & Co. was changed to a limited company under the title of Treseders' Nurseries (Truro) Limited, with Neil and his sister, Mary, as directors: Neil was the horticultural expert and specialist nurseryman, while Mary managed the office and administration. Neil eventually took over control of the business when Ira retired. This coincided with the appointment of David Knuckey, who had just completed his National Diploma of Horticulture at Wisley, as Nursery Manager. David was already familiar with Treseders': prior to his time at Wisley, he had trained at the nurseries for four years. He was chiefly responsible for propagating new plants, and the nursery cottage was provided as accommodation for him and his family. His children had the most wonderful childhood, enjoying the freedom of the nursery grounds when all the workmen had gone home.

Neil Garland Treseder.

Like Treseders past and present, Neil had many innovative, and sometimes impetuous, ideas: some worked; others did not. One of his great disappointments came in the late 1950s, and arose from a project to grow *Acacia dealbata* (mimosa). He had noticed that there was a growing demand for mimosa in the cut-flower trade, and that the mature specimens his father had planted in gardens in the Helford area of Cornwall many years previously flourished in the mild climate. Consequently, he rented some land at the end of Bar Road, on the slopes of the Helford River, and planted thousands of mimosa and eucalyptus seedlings in the hopes of making a good profit by sending flowers and foliage to Covent Garden, in London. But Neil had not realized that the mimosa sprays imported from the South of France to be sold in the Truro shop were cut from specifically grafted species. Unfortunately, as his plants were seedlings they were not vigorous enough, nor did each flower – a problem compounded by several hard winters which damaged the crops severely, so that the project had to be abandoned. However, with the growth of Interflora and the Treseder introductions of Australasian plants, the local rural economy was boosted to a certain extent. As Neil had planted mimosa on the banks of the Helford, so many families planted small strips of land on the southern banks of the River Fal with pittosporum and eucalyptus, carefully pruning the plants to encourage the growth of long stems which were then cut and packed in hessian to be sent by train to Covent Garden. Many of these small plantations have been long abandoned, but the trees have matured to provide valuable protection from the wind. In mid-February 2004, I went to find the Bar Road site: the area is now devoted to private gardens, many of which contain beautiful mature mimosa trees that were a mass of golden flowers.

Flower shows

There had always been great pride and competitive spirit in the Treseder Nurseries. Neil's great-grandfather, James, had successfully entered his vegetable and flower produce at the local horticultural shows, frequently competing against his brother Stephen. By the early 1950s, Neil decided that, in order to promote their interesting stock of rare plants, he should begin to enter shows further afield. Treseders' Nurseries were already regular and well-known exhibitors at the wonderful spring flower shows at Falmouth and Penzance, but now he began exhibiting his superb range of specialist plants at Exeter, Taunton, and the Royal Cornwall and Devon County Shows, winning numerous gold and silver medals. For many years, Neil was chairman of the horticultural section of the Royal Cornwall Show, and devoted much time and energy to his duties at a time of considerable growth in the numbers of specialist nurseries in the south-west. He always included a water feature as the focal point of the flower tent, to be enjoyed by the thousands of visitors who were eager to admire the wonderful plants that could be grown in the mild south-west climate. Throughout his long involvement with these horticultural shows, he was frequently presented to most of the members of the royal family. However, mounting shows was not without its hazards: on one occasion in those early days, there was a slight mishap on the return journey from Exeter. Coming down the hill near St David's railway station, the canvas-covered trailer became unhitched and overtook Neil's car, fortunately stopping when the wheels hit the pavement.

The Royal Horticultural Society

David Knuckey recalls that, in 1962, Neil made a snap decision to exhibit in the great autumn flower show at the Royal Horticultural Society in London – an announcement he made at the beginning of the week in which the show was to take place! This marked the first of many such London events, including the spring flower show and the prestigious Chelsea Flower Show, where Treseders' regularly won silver-gilt medals. This was, in large measure, due to David's excellent eye for plant combinations, which he later continued so successfully in his own Southdown Nurseries, and then Burncoose Nurseries. In those days, Cornwall was still 'out in the sticks' as far as communication by road to horticultural events out of the county was concerned. Exhibiting at the London shows involved a tiring 12-hour journey by car, towing a canvas-covered trailer containing all the choice plants and exhibition materials. The A30 road leading out of Cornwall was hilly and winding, and passed through the busy centres of many towns and villages. The first time Neil and David exhibited at the RHS show, they left the Truro nurseries late in the evening, arriving in London at 9 am the next morning, giving them just two hours to put together their display before opening time. Neil proudly exhibited his new heather, *Erica carnea* 'Pink Spangles' (awarded the RHS Award of Garden Merit), which he had found as a sport in the garden of a Mrs Davey at Devoran. It was the first time that this stunning hardy hybrid had been seen outside his nurseries. 'Pink Spangles' is a true bicolour, the pale lilac sepals being borne at right-angles to the deep rosy-red bells. The flowers are larger than those of any other winter-flowering heather, very pale at first in January and February, but gradually intensifying in colour as the flowers mature. Today these are familiar plants, but in the 1960s they were rare indeed.

Neil's first Chelsea entry had an orange and red theme, making good use of *Embothrium coccineum* (Chilean firebush) and his red hot poker, *Kniphofia* 'Tintagel' (which he later renamed *Kniphofia* 'Atlanta'), plants he was keen to advertise. Neil discovered this particular kniphofia outside an hotel in Tintagel, and described it in his 1972 nursery catalogue as 'a sensational plant for massing in exposed situations, especially on the coast, flowering with extraordinary freedom from late May onwards bearing brick red and sulphur yellow torches'. The following year the theme was yellow, using the new yellow rhododendrons from Caerhays. In the autumn exhibitions at Alexandra Palace, the Treseder stand made use of berried plants, hydrangeas and nerines. Their wide range of exotic species that flourished in Cornwall, unknown to many, created a sensation, making these truly exciting times.

Plant propagation and books

Camellias
In 1947, Neil's enthusiasm for horticulture was increased, and new direction given to his career when he was invited to advise on the design of a garden at Eagles Nest, Zennor. This dramatic, rugged, exposed coastal site was the home of Will Arnold-Forster, the specialist maritime horticulturist and author of the classic *Shrubs for the Milder Counties*

(1948).[1] This small, private garden was later to become renowned for its wind-tolerant plants, nestling high among the rocky outcrops on the road between St Ives and Land's End, in direct contact with the salt-laden Atlantic gales. Drawing on 100 years of Treseder experience, Neil skilfully filled the rocky landscape with the most wind-hardy shrubs available, mainly from New Zealand and the cooler, coastal parts of South America. These plants hugged the ground to provide the structure of the planting in this uniquely challenging site, creating small, sheltered pockets for other slightly less hardy shrubs – in particular, for camellias. Will Arnold-Forster was in the process of writing *Shrubs for the Milder Counties* at this time, and the two like-minded men became great friends. It was while proof-reading Arnold-Forster's work, Neil explained, that he read the sentences that inspired the new departure in his own horticultural career: 'I should like to think that this chapter would encourage the planting of ten thousand camellias, in small simple gardens as well as grand ones. For these are not simply plants for the rich man's greenhouse, as used to be supposed; they are plants for Everyman.' Through the influence of Will Arnold-Forster, camellias became one of Neil's leading specialities. Treseders' catalogue number 3 (1950) reads:

> Camellias are far hardier than is generally supposed and surely must rank as the finest of all evergreen flowering shrubs. Their main requirements are a lime-free soil (pH4–6) and partial shade, especially from early morning sun, which damages frosted or dew-laden flowers. They will thrive even on a north wall or in dense shade, but will also flourish in full sun on soils which are retentive of moisture… Young plants should be mulched in spring with peat, cow manure or spent leaves, and watering with cold tea acts as a mild fertilizer. When the craze spread to Europe at the beginning of the 1800s, many varieties were imported from Japan and China, and either lost their original names or were given European ones. Treseders found some masquerading under several names.

By the 1960s, Treseders' Nursery had in stock about 250 different varieties. Some of these were new introductions, such as 'Debbie', obtained from the New Zealand camellia specialists Duncan & Davis. Neil's own success in propagation was greatly improved by the installation of one of the first electronic mist units, which allowed precise control of humidity to give new cuttings the most favourable conditions for growth. In 1967, his increasing expertise led Edward Hyams[2] to invite him to become co-author of a book entitled *Growing Camellias* (published in 1975). In his opening chapter, Neil wrote:

> Before I go on to write about camellias themselves, I must say a little about the origins of my connection with them. Our Truro nurseries were founded by my great-grandfather in 1830. My grandfather emigrated to Australia with two of his brothers in 1857 and they were propagating and growing camellias over a century ago when they had nurseries at Ashfield, near Sydney, known as Camellia Grove where they traded under the name of Treseder Bros. My father was born at Camellia Grove, and often told me how he and his brothers used to climb down from their bedroom window through a camellia tree which was growing against the wall of the house. He also told me how they assisted in collecting specimens of Australian Tree Ferns (*Dicksonia antarctica*) from the Blue Mountains and packing them for despatch to such favoured Cornish gardens as Bosahan, Caerhays, Trengwainton and Trewidden, where many fine specimens survive to this day.
>
> My grandfather did much evangelical work among the Australian aborigines, in the course of which he travelled widely, visiting many outlying islands. In an endeavour to help the inhabitants he started a world-wide trade in their native seeds bartering building materials and household utensils for seed of the Norfolk Island Pine (*Araucaria excelsa*) and the Lord Howe Palms (*Howea belmoriana* and *H. forsteriana*) the latter being better known as Kentia Palms. All of these plants became as popular as the universal Aspidistra as house plants in Victorian times. I still possess copies of some of the correspondence relating to this trade, with details of the manner in which the seeds were packed in sealed tins for export, not only to pot-plant growers and seedsmen in Great Britain but also in Europe and America.
>
> About 1950 I became the proud possessor of one of the scarce copies of *Camellia Quest* by the well-known Australian camellia authority Professor E G Waterhouse. Imagine my delight when I came across the following under the heading 'Various Australian Seedlings'; 'Winter Cheer', a seedling found growing at the foot of 'Tricolor' at Treseder's old nursery, Alt Street, Ashfield,

and named by Mr A O Ellison. It is probably a 'Tricolor' seedling. A large showy, semi-double rosy-crimson. The Australian variety 'Thomas Treseder' a large semi-double, salmon-red, veined rose, was named after one of my great-uncles and has recently been introduced into our camellia stock from propagating material supplied by the Melbourne Botanic Gardens.

When Will Arnold-Forster died, his gardener, Percy Edwards, became Treseders' resident foreman and propagator, living in the nursery cottage with his wife, who assisted him. Gradually, during the late 1960s, Neil cut back on camellia propagation, fearing that there was overproduction. He had calculated that there were at least three nurseries and ten private estates propagating camellias on a commercial scale in Cornwall alone, which, he considered, might well lead to their overexposure within the gardening fraternity. No one, not even Neil, foresaw just how enormous the garden potential and desire for these attractive flowering shrubs was to become.

By now, David Knuckey had been promoted to Nursery Manager, and Alison Bland (later O'Connor) had taken over as Propagator. She informed me that Treseders' was the first nursery to commercially propagate *Fremontodendron* 'Californian Glory', an attractive shrub for sunny walls, bearing large golden flower cups throughout the summer. Neil's interest in particular species, she told me, often followed new fashions and customers' needs. As gardens became smaller, clients began looking for a more instant impact, so Neil turned his attention to the potentillas. Among his list of introductions are *Potentilla* 'Cornish Cream' and *P.* 'Smugglers Gold', although Alison believes that he also named *P.* 'Daydawn', *P.* 'Sunset', and *P.* 'Tangerine'. Patience, and a certain amount of good luck, are essential in growing new varieties, and these last potentillas arose because they were raised from seed – when plants of different colours grew together the bees and insects crosspollinated them, thereby producing multi-coloured seedlings.

Magnolias

In August 1967, Neil embarked on a programme of bud-grafting magnolias. He had researched this through articles in the Royal Horticultural Society's *Journal*, and personal contact with magnolia specialists, Eric Munday, an American, and K. Wada from Japan, who came to the nurseries in April of that year. By the 1970s, Treseders' Nurseries' catalogue listed over 50 different magnolias that they were propagating, making these magnificent trees more widely available to the ordinary gardener. Neil had also built up a considerable export trade to America, Japan and South Korea.

Just as his earlier enthusiasm for camellias had resulted in his book *Growing Camellias*, so his interest in magnolias was marked by the writing of another book, *Magnolias* (1978). In his introduction Neil wrote:

> For over forty years I have been growing plants and making gardens in Cornwall and elsewhere and have had many opportunities to visit and enjoy the wonderful collections of magnolias in such famous Cornish estate gardens as Caerhays, Trewithen, Trengwainton, Trewidden and Lanarth. These gardens contain many of the first raisings of magnolia species introduced by such plant hunters as George Forrest and Ernest Henry Wilson. To this list I must add Chyverton, Lanhydrock, Werrington and Antony House. My particular interest in magnolias dates back some twenty-five years (early 1950s) when the late Charles P Raffill, then Assistant Curator at the Royal Botanic Gardens, Kew, called at our Truro nurseries, shortly after visiting Caerhays and Trewithen, to see the Asian magnolias in flower. He infected me with much of his enthusiasm and persuaded me to get plants and stock them. I went to see these fantastic trees and found the sight of those huge flowers on the bare stems sensational and we often corresponded afterwards.

Neil regularly visited these magnificent gardens, as well as Scorrier House, to collect buds for grafting. There was always a great camaraderie among the horticultural enthusiasts, who nurtured and shared the new plants. In this way, the species propagated were spread around, giving them a greater chance of survival. Most of the wonderful gardens Neil mentioned are now open to the public. The old Cornish families who own them have been enthusiastic caretakers and propagators of the magnolias, together with the many beautiful camellias and rhododendrons brought back by famous plant hunters throughout the 1800s.

In another extract from his book *Magnolias*, Neil describes Treseders' own *Magnolia* 'Moresk' that is still growing in the garden of the original nursery cottage which, on the sale of the nurseries, was sympathetically renovated and modernized by Truro architect Paul Bunyan for his own home:

MAGNOLIA 'Michael Rosse'

This Magnolia is believed to have originated as one of a batch of seedlings, supposed to be of *M. campbellii alba*, which were raised at Caerhays. It reached Nymans Gardens at Handcross, Haywards Heath, Sussex, via Hillier's Nurseries at Winchester. It received an Award of Merit at a Royal Horticultural Society Show on 2 April 1968 when exhibited by the Countess of Rosse and the National Trust. The RHS Floral 'B' Committee considered it to be a hybrid of *M. sargentiana* var. *robusta*. By a remarkable coincidence an almost identical Magnolia which, it transpired, had originated in precisely the same way, was exhibited at the same show from the gardens at Windsor Great Park (*M.* 'Princess Margaret'). The tree is described by head gardener Cecil Nice as being fairly erect, with leaves resembling those of *M. campbellii*. There is a similar Magnolia growing on the south side of the cottage on our old nursery at Truro which has been given the locality name 'Moresk'. It was purchased from Caerhays prior to 1960 but, unfortunately, no record of its parentage can be found. They would have been bred between 1955 and 1960…

Magnolias, published in collaboration with the Royal Horticultural Society, was the first comprehensive work on the temperate magnolias and their hybrids since Millais' *Magnolias* (1927), which had been written at a time when many magnolia introductions had yet to flower. Neil reasoned that a book of his own would create an insatiable demand for trees of certified clones. John Bond, keeper of the gardens for the Crown estate, helped considerably with the research, which took Neil on two international expeditions. The first, in 1970, was to the USA, where he lectured to the Magnolia Society and was introduced to specialists who took him to many magnolia arboreta to experience, first-hand, the enormous flowering specimen trees. The second trip, in 1974, was a plant-hunting expedition. Because of his internationally acclaimed expert knowledge of magnolia propagation, and with the help of Carl Miller, an American Director of the Seoul Bank of Korea, Neil was invited to South Korea by the state botanist, Mr Cho.

Carl Miller lived on the Korean coast, and had established an amazing garden stocked with many rare and wonderful plants collected from local Korean habitats, and nurseries world-wide. Neil was asked to label and record these plants and redesign Miller's garden. As a guest of Mr Cho, he visited South Korea's magnolia-budding nurseries, which were producing plants for export to Japan. Neil's lengthy letters home record his excitement at seeing many wonderful and rare plants and describe a 'most sensational evergreen *Daphnephyllum macrapodum*'. He brought home some of the black berries, which germinated well, and the hardy plants eventually grew to 7m high. He visited the isolated volcanic island of Cheju Do (formerly Quelpart Island), discovering many attractive plants not then in cultivation but capable of withstanding coastal exposure, and also home to the forest tree *Magnolia kobus*. Mr Cho took him on a long and arduous plant- and seed-collecting expedition on the wild and rugged slopes of Mount Halla. With the help of a local guide, they climbed thousands of feet on uncharted terrain, covering many miles in thick fog. Neil's diary records how the two men collected seeds of the rare *Berberis quelportensis*; the dwarf Mount Halla willow, *Salix hallacuensis*, and *Acer pseudo-sieboldianum*.[3] Neil was lavishly entertained by the government of South Korea, and gave a lecture on magnolias to the state dignitaries and international ambassadors – this was especially difficult as very few of them spoke English. The seeds and cuttings he had collected were prepared and packed by the staff at the Hongming Arboretum, who issued a phytosanctuary certificate to enable them to be brought back to Cornwall, together with some Korean magnolias for Neil to propagate at his own nurseries.

Neil's second magnolia publication, *The Book of Magnolias* (1981), contained 34 illustrations of magnolias and was responsible for launching the artistic career of the famous botanical illustrator Marjorie Blamey. In April 1966, Marjorie was exhibiting some of her paintings at the Cornwall Garden Society's show in Truro. Neil was so inspired by this talented and almost unknown artist that he immediately commissioned her to paint a set of the best magnolia forms to illustrate his two books. Freshly cut magnolia flowers were gathered from the magnificent specimens growing on Cornish estates, and Marjorie had to work quickly to capture the enormous blooms in precise detail before they wilted. Neil's proudest moment came when he presented a signed copy of *The Book of Magnolias* to HM Queen Elizabeth the Queen Mother. Neil's magnolia expertise was subsequently referred to in the book *Magnolias: Their Care and Cultivation* by James Gardiner (1989), at that time Curator at the RHS Garden Wisley.

It is perhaps fitting that I should conclude this section with my own recent experience of magnolias at Caerhays. I had been trying to trace a specimen of *Camellia* 'Thomas Treseder' that was initially propagated in Australia in the late 1880s by my great-grandfather, John Garland Treseder, and named after his brother. Family papers record a specimen growing in the gardens of Caerhays Castle, Gorran, near St Austell, home of the famous *williamsii* camellias and rhododendrons. I wrote to the owner of Caerhays, Julian Williams, who kindly informed me that there had indeed been a plant at Caerhays in the early 1900s, but that he was not sure of its position. He suggested that I contact his recently retired Head Gardener, Philip Tregunna. For a while I heard nothing; then, in the second week of March 2003, Philip telephoned me and asked me to meet him at the Top Lodge gates that week. The weather was fine, but we were experiencing biting easterly gales. We met as arranged and I was privileged to drive with him along the estate drive to the castle, where we were surrounded by the tallest, most beautiful magnolia trees in full flower. It was a truly breathtaking sight: the stark trunks and branches were tipped by practically solid blocks of colour, comprising the huge petals of vast flowers, from dazzling whites and the palest of pinks, through to magenta, many emitting a delicate, heady perfume. As we walked along gravel paths, the varying levels and bends revealed other fantastic vistas. Growing at the feet of the magnolias were the *williamsii* camellias and rhododendrons. Although these are woodland gardens, all the plants are clearly labelled, and I was lucky enough to be able to see the wonderful trees in all their glory while having each one's history explained to me. Philip then directed me to walk down a sloping grass pathway between tall laurel hedges. Nestling on the sheltered slopes grew the most stunningly clear pink magnolia I have ever seen, perfect in shape and symmetry. Now I understood why he had wanted to show me Caerhays gardens at this particular time: I was standing with a quiet, unassuming, but justly proud gentleman, next to his own cultivar, *Magnolia* 'Philip Tregunna'. Although I had not found *Camellia* 'Thomas Treseder', which had been crushed by a tree blown down in a winter gale many years before, the visit was very special to me, and the gardens should not be missed by anyone interested in horticulture. Caerhays now holds the National Collection of magnolias, which consists of 40 species, 170 named cultivars, and some 250 unnamed seedlings.

Horticultural projects

Rosewarne Horticultural Experimental Station

I was able to glean further information about my father from Marshall Hutchens, Senior Lecturer in Horticulture at the Duchy College, Cornwall's College of the Countryside, formerly the Rosewarne Horticultural Experimental Station, situated on the outskirts of Camborne. He wrote to me, saying, 'You are probably beginning to realize just what a major impact Neil had on horticulture in Cornwall and his name will crop up all over the place as a keen plants-person and inspiration to many.' He went on to tell me that Neil was involved in the setting up of Rosewarne in 1951, under the auspices of the Ministry of Agriculture, Fisheries, and Food (MAFF). The site, just inland from the Cornish north coast, between Portreath and Godrevy, was chosen specifically because of its exposure to the maritime elements. Neil's expert knowledge was put to good use in the planting of wind-tolerant species to protect the small trial areas used for developing new varieties of traditional crops, on which Cornish farmers relied for their livelihoods – in particular, cauliflowers, potatoes, daffodils, lilies, and anemones. A large collection of Treseder plants still survives at Rosewarne, including *Cupressus macrocarpa* 'Goldcrest', *Elaeagnus* × *ebbingei* 'Salcombe Seedling', *Escallonia rubra* 'Crimson Spire', and *E. rubra* 'Red Hedger'.

In the mid-1990s, Neil became fascinated with hebes – attractive, flowering maritime plants – and opened the National Hebe Reference Collection at Rosewarne, with a specimen of *Hebe dieffenbachia*, offspring of which still survive. Until his death in 1996, Neil was continually cross-pollinating hebes, producing numerous speciality varieties in his new 'Wand' series. I am proud to say that I have one of the 'Wand' hebes in my garden, which I removed as a small pot-plant from my father's home shortly after his death, not realizing what it was, until Barry Champion, Head Gardener at Trelissick, visited me one day and exclaimed over it. The tall, elegant shrub appears to flower more or less continuously in mild conditions, displaying beautiful, delicately perfumed, lilac-pink racemes, up to 7cm long and terminating in a narrow point. A veritable magnet for honeybees and butterflies, it is a joy to have this plant in my garden.

St Just-in-Roseland churchyard, 1980.

St Just-in-Roseland churchyard

In 1984, the Manpower Services Commission funded a community project in the St Just-in-Roseland churchyard. An extension to the burial area was urgently needed in the ground adjoining the old churchyard, which had long since been acquired for this purpose by the Parochial Church Council. As he was now retired, Neil had the unique opportunity to become professionally involved with this old Treseders' Nursery site. He managed a team of long-term unemployed personnel, using his expert horticultural and landscaping knowledge to advise on the preservation and improvement of many of the original plants, especially the graceful rows of ancient *Trachycarpus fortunei* and the massive clump of *Gunnera manicata* in the boggy area lower down, the trees and shrubs his own grandfather had lovingly planted and among which he and his sisters had played when they were children so many years before. Neil was able to give guidance on the replanting needed to replenish the stock of interesting species, designing beautiful ponds within the churchyard, and enhancing the appeal of one of the most spectacular burial-grounds in the country. In the early 1900s, his grandfather, John, had planted *Drimys winteri*, which, because of its interesting history, particularly fascinated Neil. Commonly known as 'Winter's Bark', it is named after Drake's surgeon during the first voyage of circumnavigation. It was discovered in the Magellan Straits and was of great importance to seafarers as it has antiscorbutic properties that prevented the crew from getting scurvy. Today, it can be seen thriving in the churchyard, standing some 8–10m tall, its magnificent long glossy leaves, growing on red stems, possessing an orange-like aroma when crushed. It produces large, pendulous umbels of creamy-white orange blossoms from February through to May.

Plant introductions

Although camellias and magnolias were his speciality, a major part of Neil's horticultural achievement was in discovering and propagating new plant species, especially those with 'sport' variegation. He successfully named over 60 plants, a number of them being awarded the coveted RHS Award of Garden Merit. He grew many of these plants in his own garden on the sloping river bank adjacent to the Ponsharden Yacht Marina in Falmouth.[4] Neil always felt that Cornwall's wonderful climate and amazing intensity of sunlight brought about the subtle changes in growth, and, with his keen eye for unusual plant variation, he recognized many sports on plants growing at his family nursery or in gardens he had visited. In many instances, small cuttings from the sports took years of nurturing to propagate in large enough quantities to produce commercially. There are many fascinating anecdotes about his plant discoveries, some of which have been mentioned already; others, below, I have discovered among my father's papers.

Ceanothus arboreus 'Trewithen Blue' (RHS Award of Garden Merit)
Neil's claim concerning this introduction was that he was instrumental in naming it and introducing it to many other gardens. Each spring, George Johnstone of Trewithen, near Probus, used to invite Neil to see his wonderful magnolias at their best. On one such occasion in the late 1950s, he led Neil down to the walled garden to show him some of the new daffodils he had bred. Neil had not been there on previous visits, and was astonished to see a magnificent, large-leaved ceanothus trained against the south-facing wall. It was a mass of large, rich blue flower panicles, and completely stole his attention. It was in full bloom at least two months earlier than any other cultivar, and he immediately recognized it as a very superior form of *C. arboreus*. Neil suggested to Major

Johnstone that, if he let him propagate this fine cultivar, he would give it an appropriate name, and could always be relied upon to provide a replacement if the Trewithen plant died: hence the name *Ceanothus arboreus* 'Trewithen Blue'.

Escallonia rubra 'Crimson Spire' (RHS Award of Garden Merit) and *E. rubra* 'Red Hedger'

In 1947 Neil decided to improve the kinds of escallonia commonly used for garden hedges. From a batch of seedling-raised plants of mixed *macrantha-rubra* stock, he selected two distinct types with pronounced upright growth and good crimson flowers. The larger-leaved seedling he named 'Red Hedger', and the smaller-leaved one 'Crimson Spire'. In an article about escallonias, Marshall Hutchens (2001) commented:

> Ask a horticulturist to name one Escallonia and usually the reply will be 'Crimson Spire' or 'Red Hedger'. Both of these are *E. rubra* seedlings introduced by that marvellous Cornish nurseryman Neil Treseder, whose eye for new plants was almost mythical. Both are very similar and only an expert eye will tell them apart, but that does not matter as both perform equally well under the most extreme of conditions. Both were top rated in trials carried out at Rosewarne (Cornwall College of the Countryside) during the 1960s. Hedges formed from cuttings pushed into prepared ground can give remarkable results with 6ft (1.8m) or more in three years not uncommon. The plants are festooned with bright red flowers over a long period of time and must rate as some of the best insect-attractive plants in cultivation. *E.* 'Ingramii' is similar except for the pink colour of its flowers giving a useful colour break from red. It is as tough as *E.* 'Crimson Spire' but not quite so rampant.

Cupressus macrocarpa 'Goldcrest' (RHS Award of Garden Merit)

Cupressus macrocarpa 'Goldcrest' was saved from being discarded from a tray of one-year-old seedlings of the Monterey cypress, *Cupressus macrocarpa*, being pricked out by Tom Cocking at Treseders' nursery, Truro, in the early 1950s. Among all the other seedlings, and about 4 cm tall, it was the only one which was bright yellow, so Neil stopped Tom from throwing it away and replanted it in a pot. Two years later he had it planted out in an open, south-facing situation, by which time it had grown into an erect and compact young tree of brightest gold. Neil eventually named it 'Goldcrest' after one of the smallest British birds. Cuttings of the tree were extremely difficult to propagate then, but in the 1960s there were important advances in conifer propagation techniques, which made the process much easier with 'Goldcrest'. Neil presented one of his first plants to the Queen Mother at the Truro spring flower show, at about the time she was renovating the Castle of Mey, so it is probably still in the garden there. *Cupressus macrocarpa* 'Goldcrest' was widely admired, and generally considered to be the best golden conifer raised to that date. Subsequently mass-produced in Holland, it is nowadays raised by the tens of thousands and sold world-wide.

Myrtus luma apiculata 'Glanleam Gold' (RHS Award of Garden Merit)

This myrtus was found as a self-sown seedling during a visit to Glanleam, on Valentia Island, off the coast of Kerry, between tree-like specimens of the genus, with their conspicuous, peeling, light brown bark. Neil spotted it among thousands of other seedlings because it had beautiful variegated leaves, and when he was having tea with the owner, Col. R.L. Uniacke, persuaded him to send cuttings in early autumn and let Neil name the plant after the garden. These are extremely popular plants with garden centres, and are now widely available.

Griselinia littoralis 'Bantry Bay'

This fine plant is a sport of *Griselinia littoralis*, which Neil came across in a famous garden on Garnish Island, Ilnacullin, in Bantry Bay. It has broad, wavy-margined leaves, with extensive cream and light green midleaf variegations which streak outwards to the margins and show up well from a distance.

Both *Myrtus luma apiculata* 'Glanleam Gold' and *Griselinia littoralis* 'Bantry Bay' are featured in Charles Nelson's book, *An Irish Flower Garden* (1984), together with some other cultivars which Neil introduced and named, including *Callistemon* 'Murdo Mackenzie' and *Leptospermum scoparium* 'Rowland Bryce'.

Hydrangea seemanii

In 1973, Neil received seeds of *Hydrangea seemanii* from an American botanist who had been given them during a botanical expedition in Mexico. Neil had no record of the precise area from which the collec-

tion was made, or the donor of the seeds. He planted one of the seedlings against a low retaining wall in his Falmouth garden in May 1975,
its long glossy leaves leading him to suppose it to be tolerant of shade
as well as the drips from overhanging trees and shrubs. It grew vigor-
ously and provided good ground-cover over a considerable area. He
gave a plant to Peter Bickford-Smith, of Trevarno near Helston, and I
was informed by the Head Gardener that it was still flowering in 2003.
Neil's original seedlings of *H. seemanii* were purchased quickly by plant
enthusiasts, and it is now being propagated commercially.

The Lizard peninsula is particularly renowned for its diversity of plant
species, and Neil spent many hours plant-hunting on Goonhilly Downs,
discovering two unusual Cornish heathers, which he subsequently
named *Erica vagans* 'White Rocket' and *E. vagans* 'Cornish Cream'. While
collecting gorse seeds he noticed that one plant had a more orangey
flower than the others, and this he named *Ulex* 'January Gold'. Plants
were his life and passion. His diaries illustrate his obsession, for in-
stance, about a tiny, prostrate juniper which he had discovered hugging
the cliff on the south coast near Predannack on the peninsula. Neil
was relieved when the Ministry of Defence eventually gave him special
permission to cross their airfield and he could search for this very rare
wild plant with his great friend and fellow horticultural expert Dick
Challenor-Davies, a keen and active member of the Cornwall Garden
Society. Neil named this plant *Juniperus communis* 'Soapstone', after the
area of the cliff where soapstone can be found.

Garden style
After the Second World War, house-building was on the increase and,
from 1946 to 1970, Neil was designing modern, smaller gardens. His
garden designs usually incorporated a granite wall, invariably topped
with an evergreen hedge, and boundary hedging of either escallonia,
eucryphia, grisellinea, or variegated privet adding interest with flower or
leaf colour. He was particularly keen on using his own *Escallonia* 'Red
Hedger' and *E.* 'Crimson Spire' to create fast-growing hedges for priva-
cy. Treseders' more tolerant Australasian species, such as pittosporum,
cordyline and phormium, featured, protected by various ornamental
conifers, and planting for the more sheltered gardens included callistemon, mimosa, hardy fuschia, and hydrangeas. Camellias and small rho-

dodendrons were also important garden plants, with their early flowers providing striking colour from November through to the spring. Many of the gardens in St Mawes are particularly good examples of the influence of Neil Treseder's garden designs, and his use of Australasian and maritime plants.

The Cornwall Garden Society and the Cornwall Gardens Festival

In 1979, management of the nurseries passed to Neil's eldest son, Andrew. During his retirement, until his death in 1996, aged 83 years, Neil was probably more involved in the physical handling and cultivation of his beloved plants than when he was the managing director of the nurseries. He was kept busy writing articles for magazines, giving lectures and regularly entertaining numerous societies with gardening talks and slide shows, as well as being filmed for television in his Falmouth garden.

In his retirement years Neil became one of the longest-serving and most active supporters of the Cornwall Garden Society, providing many thousands of cuttings from his own rare plants for sale at their plant stalls. He was instrumental in widening the membership of the society to amateur gardening enthusiasts, and was persuasive in planning the layout of a 133m-long marquee for the Society's seventy-fifth show at Trelissick in 1987. The Cornwall Tourist Board had asked if the Society could do something to publicize the beauty of Cornwall in spring to visitors from home and abroad – a request that resulted in the Cornwall Gardens Festival being instituted. Horticulture was a life's passion for Neil, as it had been for his father and grandfather.

I will conclude this chapter with a note my father wrote during a moment of reflection on his life's work, possibly shortly after the death of his own father, Ira, at a time when the pressures and responsibilities of managing a large business were considerable:

> With the Nurseries there is a customer relationship which probably differs from that of any other trade or profession. There are an ever-increasing number of customers who want my time and advice whether personally or by letter. As I see it, everything seems to be becoming more and more labour intensive. This includes garden designs, flower shows, stock taking on three nurseries, the preparation and revision of catalogues and lists. Should we con-

tinue to increase our range of plants? Will my son be prepared to carry on my responsibilities? Retrospectively and after all reminiscences are retrospective, I wouldn't change my vocation. It's the most exciting and spiritually rewarding occupation in the world; where one is in closest contact with the beauties of Nature; where one has access to the finest gardens (and homes) in this Country (and abroad if desired) and contact with the nicest of people.

Notes

1 This classic book was reissued by Alison Hodge, and contains photographs of some of the interesting varieties of plants that still grow there, taken by Susanna Heron, daughter of the artist Patrick Heron, who later lived at Eagles Nest.
2 Edward Hyams lived at Hill House, Landscove, near Ashburton. He was the author of many gardening books, and Garden Correspondent for the *Illustrated London News* and the *Spectator*.
3 My research has not revealed alternative names.
4 For a list of Neil's plant introductions, see Appendix 7. Further information can be found in the *RHS A–Z Encyclopedia of Garden Plants* (2001), which has colour plates of some of the plants, and the *RHS Plant Finder 2003/2004*.

5   Andrew Garland Treseder, 1941–1983

Andrew Garland Treseder, Neil's eldest son, trained in horticulture on the assumption and understanding that he would eventually replace his father as Managing Director of Treseders' Nurseries, Truro. Throughout his early teenage years, Andrew spent most weekends and school holidays at Moresk, learning about his father's business by working alongside various nursery employees, and acquiring practical experience of the everyday procedures and responsibilities of running the nurseries. The small wage packet also brought him much-needed pocket-money. On completing his education at Truro School, he commenced his horticultural training at the Rosewarne Experimental Station, where he sought to emulate his father, who had been instrumental in creating the institution. His training continued at the world-famous Royal Horticultural Society gardens at Wisley in 1960, after which he spent a further year in Holland with the Mesman family, commercial horticultural growers and exporters at Boskoop, with a production output on a scale unknown in Cornwall. On his return to Cornwall, Andrew became understudy to his father until he was sufficiently experienced to become a director of the company.

This position, however, proved to be very problematic. During his training in Holland, Andrew had experienced horticulture on a huge scale, and realized that the market was changing rapidly. Horticulture was becoming less exclusive, and the emphasis of the trade was on producing large quantities of easily propagated, attractive plants, sales of which were directed at the mass market of young homeowners. This new generation of gardeners owned homes that were being built on smaller and smaller pieces of land. Frequently, they had little or no knowledge of horticulture, and not much more time to work on their gardens, both husband and wife going out to work. Consequently, there was greater disposable income and the desire for visually attractive 'instant impact', 'throw away' gardens. Andrew was a great visionary, and he desperately wanted Treseders' Nurseries to develop a modern, innovative garden centre outlet in the walled garden of the Moresk Nursery, with customers using the new supermarket-type trolleys in which to place their plants as they walked around. His idea was to cut back on the stock available, and offer customers a choice of just a couple of each plant species – to sell, for example, only a small selection of roses, providing perhaps four varieties in each colour. This newly developing market appeared to be moving towards buying on a whim, and away from needing professional horticultural guidance. At that time there was no other competition of this kind and, being close to the city centre, the nursery was in a prime position for people to drive in and park their cars. Sadly, but understandably, the other directors – his father and his aunt Mary – who had carried on the tradition of the specialist nurseries, did not share his enthusiasm: they could neither understand nor accept these market changes.

Moving from Moresk

By the 1950s, the Moresk site had been in continuous cultivation for well over a century, and this, together with the intensive production of vegetables at the nursery during the war years, had left the soil exhausted and the ground clogged with weeds. It had always been Andrew's responsibility to try to control the weeds by spraying them, but by the mid-1970s it was decided that it would be preferable to move the nursery to a new, much larger, more fertile site of 50 acres, and Treseders' purchased a site at Resugga Farm near St Erme, on the outskirts of Truro, where the soil was suitable for growing the specialist shrubs.

During this period, Andrew's father and aunt, who were then both in their late 60s, decided to retire. The transfer of the nursery was a long process, taking about four years: the fields had to be broken in, and the

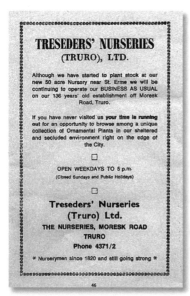

Advertisement for the move from Moresk.

whole site landscaped and ter-
raced, ready to receive plants
from the Moresk site. The
plants had to be lifted in the
correct season to survive the
move, and replanted in freshly
prepared ground. At the top of
the new nursery, a deep reservoir was excavated to provide
adequate water for irrigation,
and, adjacent to this, a large
glasshouse was constructed,
the glazing taking place during
the long, hot summer of 1976.

The new nursery was ap-
proached through a gateway
of two gigantic Chusan palms
that had been successfully

Andrew Garland Treseder, as Mayor of Truro.

transplanted after growing at Moresk for over half a century. Although
greatly abridged, Andrew's new plant catalogue included some 40 Treseder introductions. As with many small family businesses, however,
this transfer had been funded entirely out of the nursery's income, but
with little real business planning. Sadly, due to a recession in the British
economy, the land at Moresk did not sell for some time, and Treseders'
financial resources became stretched to the limit. The harsh economic
conditions coincided with the unusually severe winter of 1978/79, with
recorded temperatures of -4 – -3° C killing vast numbers of tender,
exotic shrubs in gardens throughout Cornwall.[1] Andrew lost a large
proportion of his nursery stock, and, after 150 years of trading, Treseders'
Nurseries was eventually forced to close.

However, Treseders' Interflora flower shop, which had been established in the late 1890s, continued in business. Shortly after they were
married, Andrew's wife, Marina, had trained as a florist, and together
they managed Treseders' Florists successfully with the assistance of
many talented staff. Andrew moved the business from the tiny shop
in Cathedral Lane, where Treseders' had traded for over 60 years, to
larger premises at the top of Pydar Street, with vehicular access at the
back facilitating the daily arrivals of boxes of flowers, and enabling the

careful and safe loading of beautiful bouquets, floral arrangements, and wreaths to be delivered all over Truro and the surrounding towns and villages. Shop space was urgently needed to accommodate the large chiller cabinets necessary for storing the masses of flowers required for the rapidly expanding Interflora trade. As many local wholesalers as possible were used for the supplies, including Godbers of Perranporth, Wards of Helston, and especially Johan Hicks on St Agnes, Isles of Scilly, for the season's first Paper Whites and Soleil D'Or narcissus. More exotic flowers, imported from Holland and South America, were purchased through a London agent. Floristry is an extremely labour-intensive and delicate business. On busy occasions, such as Valentine's Day, Mothering Sunday, Easter and Christmas, it was nothing to start preparing the flowers at 5 am, checking deliveries from the market against the orders, unpacking boxes and boxes of blooms, cutting stems to encourage water absorption, removing lower leaves, smashing chrysanthemum stems, de-thorning roses, and filling containers with water and 'Chrysal' to preserve them. By the 1980s, Andrew had opened another flower shop in Newquay, serving the busy hotel industry, and an outlet in the foyer of the Royal Cornwall Hospital at Treliske on the outskirts of Truro.

Truro was rapidly developing from a sleepy cathedral city to become Cornwall's commercial centre, and when the old main Post Office site at High Cross, adjacent to the main entrance of Truro cathedral, was sold to Marks & Spencer, Treseders' Florists relocated again to a newly built shop premises situated directly opposite. Business boomed for the first three years, but the city was changing. More large national chain stores were opening outlets in Truro, and shop rents were trebled with the renewal of leases, so that many small, family-run firms had to struggle hard for survival. Treseders' Florists was no exception, their situation being made worse when Marks & Spencer also began to sell flowers.

When Andrew and Marina married, they renovated and lived in the old cottage at the entrance to the Moresk nurseries, where they brought up two children, Timothy Garland and Katherine Mary Treseder. Even today, the garden of this cottage can still boast beautiful specimens of many of the wonderful, unusual plants from the family nurseries. Andrew passionately loved his home county of Cornwall, and particularly the city of Truro. He had always possessed a keen interest in public service, and was a committed member of Truro Chamber of Commerce. He could see how fast the old Truro was changing: he worked in the very heart of the city, and was always actively involved in its day-to-day life, eventually being elected to Truro City Council. Andrew had the rare ability to make everyone he met feel that their interest was of importance and worth listening to, and, in 1981, at the age of 40, he was elected Mayor, with his chosen charity being Mencap, the charity for the mentally handicapped.

Always ahead of the times with his ideas, Andrew's priority was to raise awareness of mental handicap, and he endeavoured to become the voice of people with disabilities by highlighting the problems they experienced. He was instrumental in having the kerbs lowered at pedestrian crossing points – a development which, although it may seem small, was of great importance to wheelchair-users, making their movement around the city during the course of their daily lives much easier. He also instigated the repair of the leats, so that, once again, the attractive little rivers ran through their granite gutters alongside the pavements in Truro's main streets.

At about this time, Andrew and Marina purchased a derelict farmhouse at Mylor Bridge, called Bellair Farm, once a part of the Enys estate, which contained one of the great lost gardens of Cornwall, and, by coincidence, quite near to where his great-great-grandfather, James Treseder, had established a nursery in the early 1800s. Renovation work on the house was followed by reclaiming the land of the huge, unkempt garden, in which a new wildlife pond featured.

Garden design
Like his father, grandfather, and great-grandfather before him, Andrew's deep knowledge of plants seemed to be inborn. Even though he was no longer involved in nursery work, he continued his horticultural career as a professional garden designer and lecturer, frequently giving lecture tours at the recently formed County Demonstration Gardens at Probus – this while still running Treseders' busy Interflora Florist shops in Truro, Treliske Hospital and Newquay. As garden design evolved, so Andrew's landscaping ideas evolved as well. With people wishing to spend less time maintaining, but still wanting to enjoy, their gardens, Andrew introduced more permanent garden features in his designs, and less complex planting schemes: patios and paving, balustrades and fencing, together with ground-cover such as gravel chip-

pings were incorporated into his plans. For the new generation of true garden lovers, he developed another new venture, escorting tours of the great old Cornish gardens that were gradually being opened to the public, and arranging for visitors to stay at local hotels. He also wrote weekly gardening articles for the *West Briton* newspaper. On one occasion, Andrew recalled a most interesting visit from Professor Lockwood of Southampton University, who was searching for a specimen of an insect brought to Cornwall on the hairy stems of John Garland Treseder's original commercial introductions of Australian tree ferns in the 1890s. Named after the Dorrien Smith family of Tresco Abbey, this tiny creature, *Talitrus dorrieni*, is well established in many milder parts of the country. Not unlike a sand-hopper, the species is completely terrestrial, and feeds solely on decaying vegetable matter. Not surprisingly, whenever I dig around in my own garden at Playing Place, masses of these small black 'hoppies' bounce up and down on the freshly moved soil – small reminders of the influence of my ancestors.

In March 1983, a year after Andrew completed his mayoral duties, the Treseder family was stunned by devastating news. It came at a time when all the family was busy and exhausted at the peak of preparing hundreds of bouquets for Mothering Sunday deliveries. At the age of 42, Andrew was suddenly diagnosed with an advanced stage of a rare terminal cancer. He died late that autumn at his new home in Mylor Bridge. During those few, precious, remaining months of life, he often talked about the family's involvement in horticulture in Cornwall, commenting that the climate would have been dramatically different if the county had not been planted with trees to give shelter by our predecessors, and that it could change still further if even more trees were planted. I did not completely comprehend this statement until I started my research for this book, and discovered our family's deep understanding of the necessity of providing tree-shelter to protect our wonderful, exotic Cornish gardens.

After Andrew's death, Marina published all his *West Briton* 'Argus' gardening articles as the *Cornish Garden Notebook*, with the proceeds going to the benefit of his favoured mayoral charity, Mencap, which had just obtained a residential house in Moresk Road, named 'Treseder House' in his memory. I include here some extracts from this book, which clearly illustrate the continued interest and understanding of horticulture by yet another generation of Treseders:

April 1982 – Magnolias are well represented in the large Cornish garden. Trees of up to 80 feet [24 m] can be seen at Caerhays Castle, and to nearly that height at Trengwainton. Many of the large Cornish gardens have been built up over the past 150 years by successive owners. Some plants which you will be able to see are not really suited to our average size gardens, as they will grow too large in time. However, in many cases smaller counterparts of similar appearance can be purchased. Look for the tree ferns, *Dicksonia antarctica*. Their dark brown trunks are surmounted by huge lush green fronds. My great-grandfather was instrumental for sending these over to the Cornish gardens in the late 1800s. Prince Charles was particularly interested in the tree ferns and discussed them with me on one occasion after he returned from Geelong School.

January 1983 – I was thrilled to read in the journal of the American Magnolia Society a note, written by an expatriate Englishman, who lives in Switzerland, and whose collection of magnolias must now be one of the finest in Europe. Sir Peter Smithers recounted the present I made to him of *Magnolia Iolanthe* in the spring of 1978. I had received some small pieces of bud-wood from Felix Jury in New Zealand in 1976. These were carefully worked on to seedling *M. sargentiana robusta* and a total of five young plants resulted from seven grafts. Three of these were planted out in varying conditions to be grown on and to test their hardiness. Although growth was made during the summer it failed to ripen sufficiently and perished during the following winter. Not so with Sir Peter's plant. During 1978 it made 4 ft. 6 in. [1.4 m] of growth and by the end of summer 1980 it had grown from 15 inches [38 cm] when planted, to stand 11 ft 9 in [3.6 m] overall. Large hairy buds had developed which opened to 10–11 inch [25–28 cm] diameter blooms of a good pink. Sir Peter says: "It must be said that the general effect of the small, young tree carrying between 45 and 50 enormous blooms drooping under their own weight had a staggering effect upon beholders!"

March 1983 – I took a peep at a magnificent magnolia in the Kenwyn Church area of Truro the other day. It is a form of the rare tree, *Magnolia sprengeri*, and was displaying hundreds of rich, deep, rose-red blossoms on naked branches. In the Leats, in what was once a private garden, now a car park at the rear of Messrs

Trevails, is a lovely small tree of *M. × soulangiana* 'Lennei'. A large flowered beauty which is sweetly scented, it has chalice-shaped rosey-mauve flowers up to 8ins [20 cm] across. In Tregolls Road a large plant of the star magnolia, *M. stellata*, exhibits several hundred brilliant white blooms on a low-growth bush, while in a neighbouring garden the lovely *M. × soulangiana* blossoms profusely. A short walk up Redannick Lane reveals even more magnolias.

Marina continued Treseders' Interflora Florists for another two years, but eventually had to close the business. With the influx of multiple stores, Truro had become far too expensive for small family shops, and Treseders' Florists became a casualty of progress, the close of the last branch of a business run by the same family for so many years marking the end of an era. However, the Treseders' links with horticulture in Cornwall still survive, continued by another James, the second son of my younger brother, Paul. James studied horticulture at the Duchy College, Rosewarne, and (fittingly, for a Treseder) was involved in Cornwall's latest horticultural innovation, the Eden Project, from its conception, working at the Watering Lane Nurseries, the holding area for the tropical trees and rare plants collected from around the world to stock the enormous biomes. He and his wife, Kate, continue the family tradition, running Treseders' 'Wall Cottage' Nursery near St Austell.

Note

1   'The Hard Frosts 1978–1979', *The Cornish Garden*, 1980.

Conclusion

To summarize the Treseders' skill in landscaping and identifying suitable plants for garden designs, I include an excerpt from one of John Garland Treseder's first catalogues (*c.* 1908), which identifies his artistic expertise and understanding, both of which he considered to be essential in the design and landscaping of a garden, and which were perpetuated by his successors in the Treseders' nursery business:

> In forming a Garden, however large or small, the skilful arrangements of plants in groups is unquestionably one of the important points with the landscape gardener. Dealing with a series of groups which may form a part of the boundary, these should appear from a distance as one plantation, but on nearer approach will be seen to break up into glades, ravines, bays, and grassy lanes, each group being unique. For good effect great care must be exercised in the selection of suitable Trees and Shrubs, so that the whole shall be increasingly beautiful, harmonise in colour and form, and due consideration given to the changes of Season &c.
>
> There should be graceful outline, some of the more prominent trees standing forth, others receding in a natural manner. Portions of these plantings should have bold natural swells, in other parts scarcely any trees at all.
>
> In laying out these groups there should be thoughtful care to preserve any distant landscape or seascape, town, church, or spire, indeed anything of interest; openings between the groups should be left, so that all such points may be enjoyed from the house. The selection of trees will depend upon the climate and situation.
>
> A massive long sweeping group of shrubs and trees should be introduced in the body of the work. The ground-work of these groups should, of course, be closely shorn grass, the formation of which should represent inlets, bays, recesses, rivers and lakes. There may be at least one group of rhododendrons, these should

stand in the foreground to benefit from the shelter of the hardier trees, another of azalea, another of roses, then a mixed group of trees and shrubs. Shrubs suitable for undergrowth should not be forgotten. In the central group there should be a mass of gold falling into the lap of green, while the silver-leafed trees can be planted to appear from a distance like running brooks, and snow-clad hills. The spring, summer and autumn tints must have due care. It is this part of the landscape Gardener's work that calls forth all the qualities of the Artist. A delicate perception of the beautiful in nature with a fertile imagination, are alike essential. In this work Nature has to be followed closely, and no mind that is not particularly alive to her most secret and subtle charms can enter here with any great success.

If the Pleasure Garden be planted with due regard to pictur-esque effect, you are enchanted at every step, and by irresistible fascination led on to explore. It is hard to choose which way to take, for at each turn there is something fairer and more beautiful still.

There is ample for days, for weeks, for years, but when you have no more than just entered upon the loveliness of these scenes, you find the time has insensibly fled, and have to tear yourself away.

And this our life exempt from public haunt
Finds tongues in trees, books in the running brooks,
Sermons in stones, and good in everything – Shakespeare

FINIS

Gardens Designed & Planted
Orchards Planted by Contract
Roseries Planted and Designed
Landscape Gardening a Speciality
Roses packed to travel any distance
Rose gardens Designed and Planted
Prompt Attention given to all Orders
Please address all Letters to the Firm
Designs supplied for making Gardens
Roses packed carefully for Rail or Post
Special Quotations for Large Quantities
Orders will receive our Personal attention
Selections of Flowering Plants and Shrubs
We have a fine show of beautiful Tree Ferns
Roses securely packed to travel any distance
We grow most of our Climbing Roses in pots
Designs Furnished to Large or Small Gardens
Raffia, the best Tying Material 1/- per pound
Grand Selection of Flowering Plants and Shrubs
Cover Walls and Unsightly Places with Climbers
Extra size Specimens can be supplied of all the Conifers
Any of the Fir Tribe not mentioned here can be supplied
Catalogue of Perennial Flowering Plants & Alpines on Application
Let us know the nature of your soil and we will advise what to plant
For Green Fly on Roses use Treseder's Insecticide 6d. & 1/- bottle
If you receive two Catalogues – give your Neighbour one
Advice given freely as to soil and position for Fruit Trees
Our Advice Freely Given, inquiries by post solicited
We depend upon the recommendation of our friends
Fruit Trees packed carefully to travel any distance
Send us a Trial Order and you will be pleased
Visitors are always welcome at our Nurseries
Rare Hardy Shrubs and Trees a Speciality
Plants packed carefully for Rail or Post
Our Nurseries are worthy of a Visit.

*

*

Treseder & Co. Professional Landscape Gardeners
Treseder & Co., Garden Architects, TRURO
Treseder & Co., Rose Growers, TRURO
Treseder & Co., The Nurseries TRURO
Treseder& Co., Nurserymen, TRURO
Treseder & Co. Landscape Gardeners
Treseder & Co., Seedsmen, TRURO
Treseder & Co.'s. Beautiful Ferns

Advertising tags from Treseder & Co. catalogue, c. 1900.

Appendices

Appendix 1: Plants Exported to Bosahan from Australia, 1890

This list, dated July 1890, has been transcribed from a hand-written shipment ledger from the Sydney nurseries. Current names of plants are given where known.

Shipment of plants from Australia on SS Ormuz *to A. Pendarves Vivian of Bosahan, Helford, Cornwall.*

Qty	Plant name (1890)	Plant name (2004)	Price £. s. d.
2	*Alsophila excelsa*	*Cyathea Howeana*	4. –
2	*Alsophila grandis*	*Cyathea brownii* (Norfolk Island)	4. –
2	*Kentia Forsteriana*	*Howea forsteriana*	3. –
1	*Kentia Canterburyana*	*Hedyscepe canterburyana*	1. 6
20	*Areca Baueri* in store pot	*Rhopalostylis baueri*	5. –
20	*Areca Sapida* in store pot	*Rhopalostylis sapida*	5. –
20	*Kentia Belmoriana* in store pot	*Howea belmoreana*	10. –
16	*Araucaria excelsa*	*Araucaria columnaris*	10. –
2	*Araucaria excelsa* large plants	*Araucaria columnaris*	10. –
1	*Araucaria bidwillii*	*Araucaria bidwillii*	1. 6
1	*Araucaria Cookii*	*Araucaria columnaris*	2. –
16	*Corypha Australis* in store pot	*Livistona australis*	5. –
6	*Dicksonia Antarctica* 8ft	*Dicksonia Antarctica*	4. 4. –
15	*Dicksonia Antarctica* 1, 2, & 3ft	*Dicksonia Antarctica*	2.18. –
1	*Alsophila Australis* 8ft	*Cyathea australis*	14. –
28	*Seaforthia elegans*	*Ptychosperma elegans*	5. –
1	*Pittosporum eugenioides* Variegata	*Pittosporum eugenioides* 'Variegatum'	1. 6

1	*Pisonia grandis*	*Pisonia grandis*	1. 6
1	*Stenocarpus cunninghamii*	*Stenocarpus cunninghamii*	1. 6
1	*Laganaria Pattersonii*	*Lagunaria patersonii*	1. 6
1	*Eucalyptus ficifolia*	*Eucalyptus ficifolia*	2. –
1	*Bankinia Alba*	*Banksia alba*	2. –
1	*Lophostemon Australis*	*Lophostemon tristania*	1. 6
1	*Sterculia heterophylla*	*Cola heterophylla*	1. 6
2	*Ceratopetalum gummiferum*	*Ceratopetalum gummiferum*	3. –
2	*Castanospermum australis*	*Castanospermum australis*	3. –
2	*Telopia speciosissima*	*Telopea speciosissima*	3. –
1	*Maratia elegansa*	*Marattia salicina* (Norfolk Island)	3. –
2	*Phormium colensoi* Variegata	*Phormium cookianum*	3. –
3	*Jasminium Didymum* (store pot)	*Jasminum lineare*	2. 3
2	*Iris Robinsoniana*	*Moraea robinsoniana*	3. –
2	*Doryanthus excelsa*	*Doryanthes excelsa*	3. –
1	*Dracaena canaefolia*	*Cordyline sp*	1. 6
1	*Dracaena nutans*	*Cordyline sp*	1. –
1	*Aralia reticulata*	*Meryta denhamii*	1. 6
1	*Barleleya syringaefolia*	?	2. –
	Collection of Australian native seeds		1. 0. 3
1	Wardian case		1.10. –
	Insurances and other charges		2.14. 6
			£18. 9. –

Appendix 2: Seeds and Plants Exported from Australia, 1890–93

The following list, taken from John Garland Treseder's hand-written Australian shipment ledger, covers most of the seeds and plants he was exporting world-wide during the years 1890–93. Entries marked with an asterisk (*) indicate a name used in 1890 which is not identifiable with current horticultural nomenclature.

Exported as seed:

Actinotus helianthi

Araucaria columnaris

A. heterophylla

Archontophoenix alexandrae

A. cunninghamiana

Boronia serrulata

Clianthus formosus

Cordyline stricta

Dicksonia antarctica

Doryanthes excelsa

Dracaena Cannaefolia *

D. Nutans *

Eucalyptus bicolour

E. citriodora

E. ficifolia (Red Gum)

E. globulus

E. haemostoma

E. paniculata

Ficus rubiginosa 'Australis'

Grevillea robusta

Hedyscepe canterburyana

Howea belmoreana

H. forsteriana

Kennedia rubicunda

Kentia Moorii *

Livistona australis

Moraea robinsoniana

Phormium tenax 'Variegatum'

Pinus radiata (Grass Pine of California)

Pittosporum undulatum

Ptychosperma elegans

Rhopalostylis baueri

R. sapida

Sincarpia laurifolia

Telopea speciosissima

The following were also exported as plants:

Alsophila excelsus

Araucaria columnaris

Blandfordia grandiflora

Chamaecyparis lawsoniana

Cordyline australis 'Aureo-lineata'

C. stricta

Cyathea dealbata

C .medullaris

C. smithii

Dicksonia antarctica

Doryanthes excelsa

Macrozamia spiralis

Pinus sylvestris

Platycerium bifurcatum

Appendix 3: Plants Shipped from Treseders' Nurseries, Truro, to Hobart Public Gardens, via Sir Philip Fysh, Agent General for Tasmania, November 1899

This list is transcribed from a hand-written nursery letter, in which John Garland Treseder also suggests the planting of Californian Redwood to naturalize in the Tasmanian forests.

12 Maple – Scarlet
13 Maple – Japanese
12 [? Maple]
12 *Chamaerops humilis*
6 *Trachycarpus fortunei*
50 Larch – *Larix deciduas*
10 Copper Beech (*Fagus sylvatica* Cuprea Group)
10 Silver Birch
10 Golden drooping Birch
5 Lime drooping
4 Ash drooping (various)
5 *Aucuba japonica* 'Variegata'
2 *Catalpa bignonioides* 'Aurea'
6 *Chionanthus virginicus*
3 *Choisya ternate*
3 *Chaenomeles speciosa* – 3 new varieties
3 *Cytisus scoparius* 'Andreanus'
2 *Juglans regia*
3 *Koelreuteria paniculata* (golden leaves in autumn)
4 *Kalmia latifolia*
2 *Magnolia tripetala* – Umbrella Tree
3 Golden leaf poplar
6 Rhododendrons – Indian varieties
6 *Rhus glabra* 'Laciniata'
6 *Cotinus coggygria*
6 *Sambucus nigra f. laciniata*
3 Lilacs – new large kinds
3 *Viburnum plicatum*

2 *Viburnum plicatum f. tomatosum*
2 *Parthenocissus tricuspidata*
6 Corylus (purple leaf Filbert)
2 *Acanthus hungaricus* (immense leaves)
3 *Gunnera tinctoria*
3 *Embothrium coccineum*
50 Strawberry 'Royal Sovereign'
2 Escallonia sp. (sweet scented)
2 *Buddleja lindleyana*
6 *Clematis terniflora* (yellow)
4 *Passiflora caerulea* 'Constance Elliott'
2 *Wisteria frutescens* 'Magnifica'
24 Canna – new orchid kinds
3 *Macleaya cordata*
6 *Gypsophila paniculata*
4 *Helleborus orientalis*
20 *Iris orientalis* (The Orchid Iris)
50 Crocosmia (assorted)
2 Paeonia (the new kinds light cream/pink)
10 *Physalis alkekengi* var. *franchetii*
11 Californian Violet (new very large)
3 Rose – The Crimson Rambler
2 Rose – The Yellow Rambler
3 *Chamaecyparis lawsoniana* 'Lutea'
2 *Desfontainea spinosa*
12 Raspberry superlative (abundant leaves – 4 times larger than any other)

Appendix 4: Early Australasian Introductions

The following extract is taken from one of the earliest Treseders' catalogues, *c.* 1904.

NEW ZEALAND AND AUSTRALIAN PLANTS
And others which will thrive in Cornwall and South Devon

The question is naturally asked what will grow in my garden? Well, if it is below the 30th parallel on the South Coast, where the influence of the Gulf stream is felt, it is really wonderful what will succeed out of doors if planted judiciously. In a Torquay garden, the *Livistona australis*, *Phoenix canariensis*, *Dicksonia antarctica* are quite at home. The *Pittosporum undulatum*, *Abutilons* and *Heliotropes* are not in the least affected during winter.

Coming further South, at Salcombe the Banana has fruited outside. The Bougainvillea has stood the winters, and the Swainsona is not at all unusual, while the *Acacia dealbata* and *baileyana* grow into trees, which are covered with flowers during the winter months. Then, again, at Falmouth and district the same thing applies. At "Carclew" the *Dicksonias* are perfectly hardy, and at "Trebah" on the Helford River, *Acacias*, etc, grow away into trees. Of course tact and judgement are necessary in the planting, but there is no reason why, on entering a part of every garden, one could not imagine oneself in New Zealand and Australia.

Acacia baileyana	*C. ventricosa*
A. dealbata	*Embothrium coccineum*
A. melanoxylon	*Grevillea glabrata*
Boronia megastigma	*G. sulphurea*
Brachychiton populneus	*Luma apiculata*
Brachyglottis repanda	*Pittosporum eugenioides*
Calamagrostis arundinacea	*P. eugenioides* 'Variegatum'
Callitrus rhomboidea	*P. ralphii*
Casuarina quadrivalis	*P. tenuifolium* 'Nigricans'
C. torulosa	*P. undulatum* (Australian Daphne)
Clianthus puniceus 'Albus'	*Senecio petasitis*
Correa alba	*Senna corymbosa*
C. bicolour	*Solanum aviculare*
C. curiosa.	*Sophora tetraptera*
C. magnifica	*Swainsona galegifolia* 'Albiflora'

Appendix 5: Varieties of Eucalyptus and other Australasian Plants at Treseders' Nurseries, Truro, 1905

This list is transcribed from a Treseders' Nurseries letter book of 1905. Entries marked with an asterisk (*) indicate a name used in 1905 which is not identifiable with current horticultural nomenclature.

Eucalyptus varieties

E. acmenioides

E. affinis

E. amygdalina

E. baileyana

E. bicolor

E. botryoides

E. bridgesiana

E. camphora

E. capitellata

E. citriodora

E. coriacea

E. corymbosa

E. crebra

E. Deanii

E. enge *

E. eximia

E. globulus

E. Gunnii

E. lonfigolia

E. maculata

E. melliodora

E. microcorys

E. obliqua

E. paniculata

E. piperata

E. platyphylla

E. polyanthemos

E. pulverulenta

E. punctata

E. redunca

E. regnans

E. resinifera

E. resinifera var. grandiflora

E. saligna

E. selmonphloria *

E. stellulata

E. tereticornis

E. viminalis

Australasian plants

Acacia baileyana

A. dealbata

A. decurrens

Alphitonia excelsa

Brachychiton acerifolius

B. populneus

Callistemon lanceolatus

Callistris rhomboidea

Casuarina cunninghamiana

C. glauca

C. gradularia *

C. nana *

C. torulosa

Ceratopetalum gummifirum

Congosphorea cordifolia *

Echinocarpus australis *

Endiandra glauca

Eugenia smithii

Ficus macrophylla

F. rubiginosa 'Australis'

F. rubiginosa 'glauca'

Glemina leicharedti *

Lophostemon confertus

(Australasin plants, continued)
Tristama sucreolens *
Melaleuca leucadendra
Melia composita
M. nana *
Phyllanthus ferdinandi

Podocarpus salignus
Slaecarpus cyanens *
S. sucreolens *
Syncarpia laurifolia
Tylomelum pyriforme

Appendix 6: Rare Plant Introductions, c. 1911

By 1911, Treseder & Co.'s catalogue 'List of Novelties' had changed dramatically, with plants being introduced from throughout the world. The following list comprises a few rare plants found to be hardy in Cornwall and many other favoured places in England.

Abelia floribunda
Acer negundo ssp. *californicum* 'Aureum'
Ailanthus altissima
Amorpha canescens
Aralia spinosa
Berberis manipurana
Berberis thumgbergii
Brachyglottis repanda
Buddleja albiflora
Buddleja asiatica
Buddleja colvillei
Buddleja davidii var. *magnifica*
Caesalpinia japonica
Calamagrostis arundinacea
Carpenteria californica
Cassinia leptophylla subsp. *Vauvilliersii*
Corokia buddlejoides
Cotinus coggygria 'Rubrifolius Group'
Cotoneaster angustifolia

Cotoneaster franchetti
Crinodendron hookerianum
Escallonia bifida
Eucalyptus bridgesiana
Fallopia baldschuanica
Hedysarum multijugum
Jasminum mesnyi
Jovellana violacea
Mahonia aquifolium × *pinnata*
Nandina domestica
Philadelphus 'Manteau d'Hermine'
Pieris formosa
Romneya coulteri
Sambucus racemosa 'Plumosa Aurea'
Solanum crispum
Stephanandra tanakae
Tamarix ramosissima 'rubra'
Teucrium fruticans
Trachelospermum jasminoides
Viburnum cassinoides
Xanthoceras sorbifolium

Appendix 7: Treseder Plant Introductions

Entries marked with an asterisk (*) received the RHS Award of Garden
Merit. Current plant names/synonyms are given in square brackets.

John Garland Treseder

Camellia japonica 'Thomas
  Treseder' (Australia, c. 1890)
Dracaena tresederiana [Cordyline]
Eucalyptus beauchampiana
  [E. bridgesiana]

Ira Garland Treseder

Cosmos atrosanguineus [Bidens
  atrosanguinea] *
Populus candicans 'Aurora'
  (x jackii) *

Neil Garland Treseder

Abutilon × suntense 'Amethyst'
A. × suntense 'Minuet'
A. × suntense 'Violetta'
A. × suntense 'White Swan'
Agapanthus campanulatus
  'Ultramarine'
Aucuba japonica 'Goldenheart'
Berberis × stenophylla 'Lemon
  Queen'
B. × stenophylla 'Pink Pearl'
Buddleja davidii 'Royal Red
  Variegated'
B. fallowiana 'Bishop's Violet'
B. fallowiana 'Lavender Haze'
B. globosa 'Lemon Ball'
Callistemon 'Murdo MacKenzie'
Camellia japonica 'Altheaflora
  Gigantea' *
C. japonica 'Wally Abbis'
Ceanothus arboreus 'Trewithen
  Blue' (ex Trewithen, 1956) *

C. thyrsiflorus 'Prostratus'
Chaenomeles 'January Pink'
  (cathayensis × lagenaria)
Chamaecyparis lawsoniana
  'Ellwoods Gold' *
Cupressus macrocarpa 'Goldcrest' *
Cytisus albus 'Early White Spire' *
C. scoparius 'Gew Graze'
Elaeagnus × ebbingei 'Salcombe
  Seedling'
E. pungens 'Golden Lining'
E. pungens 'Silver Lining'
Erica carnea 'Pink Spangles' *
E. cinerea 'Heathfield'
E. terminalis stricta 'Thelma
  Woolner'
E. vagans 'Cornish Cream' *
E. vagans 'White Rocket'
E × watsonii (ciliaris × tetralix)
Escallonia macrantha 'Bantry Bay'
E. rubra 'Crimson Spire' *
E. rubra 'Red Hedger'
Eucryphia × 'Penwith' billardieri
  (lucida) × moorei
Griselinia littoralis 'Bantry Bay'
Hebe × franciscana 'White Gem'
H. glaucophylla 'darwiniana
  Variegata'
H. glaucophylla 'Variegata'
H. 'Harlequin'
H. 'Mrs Penna'
H. Wand Series: 'Bicolor Wand',
  'Blush Wand', 'Lilac Wand',
  'Pink Wand', 'Violet Wand',
  'White Wand', Blue Wand'

Hydrangea seemanii
Juniperus communis 'Gew Graze'
J. communis 'Soapstone'
Kniphofia 'Atlanta'
Leptospermum scoparium
   'Boconnoc'
L. scoparium 'Rowland Bryce'
Myrtus luma apiculata 'Glanleam
   Gold' *
Olearia albida × *haastii*
Osteospermum ecklonis 'Blue Streak'
Passiflora × *tresederi* 'Lilac Lady'
   (caerulea × *caerulea-racemosa)*
P. × *tresederi* 'Telstar'
Pittosporum tenuifolium 'Tresederi'

Potentilla 'Cornish Cream'
P. 'Smugglers Gold'
Prunus laurocerasus 'Green Marble'
Pyracantha augustifolia 'Christmas
   Cheer'
Rosmarinus officinalis 'Corsicus
   Prostratus'
R. officinalis 'Fota Blue'
R. officinalis 'St Mawes Hybrid'
Skimmia japonica 'Redruth'
Ulex europaeus 'January Gold'
U. europaeus 'Scilly Gold'
Vibernum tinus 'Port of Nice'
V. tinus 'Spring Beauty'

Bibliography

Treseder family papers and nursery catalogues
1886–1920 Diaries of John Garland and Mary Beauchamp Treseder
1888–1894 John Treseder's Australian Shipment and Export Ledgers
1888–1921 John Treseder's Australian and Truro Nurseries copy letters
1900–1979 Treseders' Nurseries, Truro catalogues – various.
Letters, memoirs and articles written by John Garland Treseder, Ira Garland Treseder, Neil Garland Treseder and Marie Louise Treseder

References
This list gives details, as available, of published works referred to.

Anonymous (1980) 'The Hard Frosts 1978–1979', in *The Cornish Garden: The Journal of the Cornwall Garden Society*, no. 23, pp. 24–5.
Arnold-Forster, W. (1948), *Shrubs for the Milder Counties*. London: Country Life. 2nd edn., Penzance: Alison Hodge, 2000.
Betjeman, J. (1964), *Cornwall: A Shell Guide*. London: Faber & Faber.
Chittenden, F.J. (ed.), Synge, P.M. (ed.) (2nd edn), (1951), *RHS Dictionary of Gardening*, 4 vols + supplement. Oxford: Clarendon Press.
Cornwall Gazette, 1 February 1839.
Gardeners' Chronicle, July 1905, p. 3; 17 March 1906, p. 174. London: Gardeners' Chronicle.
Gardiner, J. (1989), *Magnolias: Their Care and Cultivation*. London: Cassell.
Hora, Bayard (1981), *Oxford Encyclopedia of Trees of the World*. Oxford: Oxford University Press.
Hutchens, M. (2001), 'Escallonias', in *The Cornish Garden: The Journal of the Cornwall Garden Society*, no. 44, p. 8.
Jellicoe, G., Jellicoe, S., Good, P. & Lancaster, M. (1986), *The Oxford Companion to Gardens*. Oxford: Oxford University Press.
Johnson, H. (1973), *The International Book of Trees*. London: Mitchell Beazley.
Kemp, E. (1850), *How to Lay Out a Garden*. London: Bradbury & Evans.
Loudon, J. C. (1822), *An Encyclopaedia of Gardening*. London: Longmans.
— (1830), *Gardeners' Magazine*. London

Lubbock, B. & Spurling, J. (1972), *The Best of Sail*. Cambridge: Patrick Stephens.

McMillan Browse, P. (1986, Fall), 'Rosemaries', in *Pacific Horticulture*.

Millais, J.G. (1927), *Magnolias*. London: Longmans, Green.

Nelson, E. C. (1984), *An Irish Flower Garden*. Kilkenny: Boethius Press.

Payton, P. (1999), *The Cornish Overseas*. Fowey: Alexander Associates.

Pontey, W. (1822), *The Rural Improver; Or, A Practical Treatise on the Nature and Management of Such Rural Scenes and Objects, as are Necessary to Promote the Comfort, Convenience, and Embellishment of the Residences of the Higher Ranks of Society*. London: John Harding.

Royal Cornwall Gazette, 27 January 1882.

Royal Horticultural Society (1956) *RHS Dictionary of Gardening*, no.2, p. 677. Oxford: Oxford University Press.

— (2002), *The RHS Plant Finder 2003–2004*. London: Dorling Kindersley.

Royal Horticultural Society (2003), *RHS A–Z Encyclopedia of Garden Plants*. London: Dorling Kindersley.

Sackville-West, V. (1953), *In Your Garden Again*. London: Michael Joseph.

Savige, T.J. (1993), *The International Camellia Register*. Sydney: The International Camellia Society.

Smithers, P. (1995) *Adventures of a Gardener*. London: Harvill Press with the RHS.

Thurston, E. (1930), *British and Foreign Trees and Shrubs in Cornwall*. Cambridge: Cambridge University Press for Royal Institution of Cornwall.

Treseder, A. (1985), *Cornish Garden Notebook*. Truro: Radcliffe Promotions.

Treseder, J. & Treseder, T. (1882), *The Garden: A Simple Treatise in Gardening Applicable to the Seasons of this Colony*. Sydney.

Treseder, N. (1978), *Magnolias*. London: Faber & Faber in collaboration with the RHS.

— (1981), *The Book of Magnolias*. London: Collins.

— (1987), 'Some Treseder Novelties and Introductions', *The Cornish Garden*: The Journal of the Cornwall Garden Society, no. 30, pp. 62–165.

Treseder, N. & Hyams, E. (1975), *Growing Camellias*. London: Thomas Nelson & Sons.

Visick, J. (2004), *Travelling Trees – From the Wild to the West: 200 Years of Plant-Hunting*. Truro: Royal Cornwall Museum. (Catalogue for an exhibition celebrating the 200th anniversary of the RHS.)

Waterhouse, E.G. (1947), *Camellia Quest*. Sydney: Ure Smith.

Index